Stories About Teaching, Learning, and Resilience

NO NEED TO BE AN ISLAND

• • •

Steve Piscitelli

The Growth and Resilience Network™

Library of Congress Cataloging-in-Publication Data: 2016956918
The Growth and Resilience Network, Atlantic Beach, FL

ISBN 0998258504
eISBN 9780998258508
Printed in the United States
CreateSpace
The Growth and Resilience Network™

First Edition

Also by Steve Piscitelli

Choices for College Success
Study Skills: Do I Really Need This Stuff?

To my teaching colleagues around the world.

A FEW REASONS TO CONSIDER THIS BOOK

• • •

One of the benefits of teaching is that each day when we enter the room with our students, we close the door and "do our thing!" One of the greatest challenges of teaching is that each day when we enter the room with our students, we close the door and "do our thing!" You see, the freedom to "do our thing," be creative, and "spin our magic" within the classroom comes with a price if we do not remain mindful. We can become isolated. We can get lulled into the mind-set that we are an island, separate from our colleagues. And we can lose the power and strength of what a united teaching and learning community can bring to us. With the scenarios in this book, Steve Piscitelli will help you promote collegial conversations and strategies for personal and professional resilience. There is no need to be an island.

What colleagues have said concerning **Stories about Teaching, Learning, and Resilience: No Need to be an Island**

> *I think it's brilliant. I often feel like I'm on an island as a professor. I wish I'd had something like this when I first started teaching over 20 years ago...The scenarios really help get the reader into the discussion and prepared to think about the issue at hand.*
>
> —*Ashli Archer, Professor*

> *This is a fantastic project and the book will be a welcome resource! I certainly can think of ways to incorporate it into the work our office does here!*
>
> —*Todd Stanislav, Director, Faculty Center for Teaching and Learning*

I think this is a wonderful idea and have never seen anything along these lines before!

> *—Mary Boone Treuting, Professor of Psychology*
> *and Director of Center for Academic Success*
> *and the Center for Teaching Excellence*

I like how you let people know that even though you have developed a table of contents, they might want to skip around. The flexibility will be very appealing.

> *—Erin Hoag, VP of Financial Services and Strategic*
> *Development, Innovative Educators*

Your scenario addressing the issue of favoritism vs. jealousy demonstrates amazing insight and ability to address the "hard" topics. Bravo!

> *–Karen Armstrong, Career Counselor*

Wow, you are covering some controversial topics! This book is going to be different and invaluable!

> *—Pam Ranallo, Co-Owner, Innovative Educators*

Contents

Go to www.stevepiscitelli.com for supporting video.

Categorical Listing of Scenarios
Accommodations

Balance and Well-Being

Can We Talk?

• • •

Organizing Question: How can a scenario-based approach to teaching and learning efficacy stimulate meaningful conversation on your campus about growth and resilience?

Go to www.stevepiscitelli.com for supporting video.

RESILIENCE

SIMPLY PUT, "RESILIENCE" REFERS TO our adaptability in difficult situations. Riffing off an old cliché, when life throws lemons at us and knocks us off-balance, the resilient ones among us not only get up, but they gather up the lemons and figure out what they can do with their newfound resource. They are more apt to see the setbacks or failures as opportunities. This does not mean they are Pollyanna, always smiling and cheerful. No, they can feel the sting of disappointment, heartache, and pain like any of us.

Our resilient friends, colleagues, and family members, though, seem to have a better chance at picking themselves up, regulating their responses, and moving forward. Sometimes they go in new directions; at other times they recalibrate with their newfound feedback and continue on with a renewed sense of grit. In either case, they grow as a result of their experience. The resilient person lying in a pile of lemons not only gets up and makes lemonade; he or she might decide it's time for him or her to build a lemonade stand, find some investors, and become an entrepreneur. Failure and disappointment lead him or her forward. He or she remains in a learning mode and summons the grit to continue his or her journey.

While this book won't give you the secret mixture for a successful lemonade stand, it will remind you that every teaching and learning situation—everyone—gives you the opportunity to take stock of your own resilience level and build it ever stronger. And you don't have to do it alone. That's the beauty of our calling!

No Need to Be an Island: The Power of Collaboration

One aspect of my day-to-day campus teaching that I enjoyed was that each time I entered the room with my students, I could close the door and "do my thing"!

One of the greatest challenges of my day-to-day campus teaching was that each time I entered the room with my students, I could close the door and "do my thing"!

You see, the freedom to "do my thing" and be creative and "spin my magic" within the classroom comes with a price. If we do not remain mindful, we can, over time, become isolated. We can easily get lulled into the mind-set that we are an island, separate from our colleagues. And we can lose the power and strength of what a united teaching and learning community can bring to us.

When Tony Hsieh moved the Zappos headquarter to Las Vegas, he limited the number of entrances and exists for the building. This better orchestrated a flow to encourage "collisions" and accelerate serendipity among the employees.[1]

We lose that serendipity in teaching when we choose to wall ourselves off from our colleagues. This self-imposed isolation could have untold negative repercussions on our teaching, student learning, and on our personal and collegial resilience.

You have a great deal to share with your colleagues. And they have a great deal to share with you. Basketball coach Mike Krzyzewski (Coach

K) of Duke said that successful teams play like a fist: the individual fingers represent communication, trust, collective responsibility, care, and pride.[2] The same can be said for a collegial teaching and learning community.

This book can promote collegial conversations about teaching, learning, and your personal resilience—especially when you use it for discussion starters with your colleagues.

Collaboration and communication are powerful forces for personal resilience and professional growth. They lead to clarification (not justification) and edification (not pontification). There is no need to be an island.

Let's Have a Conversation

After I am contacted by any institution, company, or group to work with their teams, one of the first things I do is reach out with a simple question: "Can we talk?" I must totally understand what the contracting entity needs—and that I'm the correct fit for the event or group.

A few things prove consistent no matter where I go in this nation.

- I hear, "Give us practicality." The groups want **RELEVANCE**. Rather than being buried in data and statistics, they want practicality and immediate applicability.
- I hear, "Talk with us." The groups welcome my efforts to visit with audience members and begin meaningful conversations. They appreciate that I establish a **RELATIONSHIP** rather than give a talk and walk away.
- I hear, "There is a morale issue, a trust issue. We have attitudes that need to change." Attitudes walk into any room I am in—and attitudes walk out of those rooms. The chances of me changing "attitudes" (long-held beliefs and habits) are slim. The challenge I readily accept, though, allows me to facilitate a conversation so that once I leave the team, the members will continue talking. This makes my job one of emphasizing **RELEVANCE**, **RESPONSIBILITY**, and **RELATIONSHIPS**.

- I hear, "We would like to focus on skill development." There is a lot of "training" attention devoted to technique, technology, and, unfortunately, tautology. Often, little more than lip service (I have found in my experiences) goes to personal well-being for the faculty, staff, and administration. Without a focus on **RESILIENCE**, the institution is delusional if it thinks its people will get better. They may get worse—or even leave the institution. When that happens, think of it as a **RESOURCE** walking off campus.

- I ask, "Who are your all-stars?" Decades ago I was told about the apocryphal adage that "an expert is anyone who comes from more than one hundred miles away." I always ask about the local "experts"—those faculty who are making a difference and inspire their colleagues. Every campus has its true ALL-STARS. Some people know these people; many don't recognize the **RESOURCE** they are for their campus, students, and colleagues. Let's give them the stage! (See the exercise in the Introduction later in this book.)

- I ask, "Have faculty been asked to help plan this event that is for them?" More times than not, faculty have not had regular and meaningful input into the training that is created for them—and that they are mandated to attend. If leadership misses the opportunity to **REFLECT** upon proper faculty input, **RELEVANCE** may be sacrificed. Faculty, even the most jaded, have their **RAINBOWS**. How can we tap into these dreams and use them for everyone's benefit?

Why Not a Faculty Focus?

Higher education rightfully focuses upon the resilience of its student body. The students, after all, are the reason for higher education's existence—our reason for being.

I propose, we shift the spotlight to our faculty (and by extension, to our staff and administration). This book's intent—my intent—is to initiate a conversation that allows you to talk about issues that matter for faculty. And, ultimately, when we do that, we end up talking about issues that matter for our students.

It's time for a faculty-resilience focus. If your institution already pays homage to and readily supports faculty-growth opportunities, I congratulate you and urge you to build on this momentum. Don't let it wane. If your institution struggles with this, then allow the following pages to get that conversation started. Whatever your workplace culture may be, after we get the conversation started, I want to get out of your way. This book provides the tools for continued meaningful collegial interactions.

As emphasized in the bullet points above, I will use the seven Rs for success (relationships, relevance, resources, rainbows, responsibility, reflection, and resilience) as the basic framework of the book. (See the Introduction for an in-depth description.)

THE STORIES WE LIVE: SCENARIO-BASED TEACHING AND LEARNING

Teaching can become an insular calling with us going from our office to the classroom and back. And if repeated over a semester, years, and a long career, we can become myopic.

This book can help you and your colleagues to take incremental steps toward ongoing dialogue—true dialogues as contrasted with collective monologues where everyone talks and few listen.

As the title of this book states, there is no need to be an island.

Drawing on more than three decades of classroom teaching, face-to-face national workshops, webinars, and podcasts, I have found that stories (based on reality) provide an effective jumping-off point for discussion, teaching, learning, and collaboration.

The scenarios that follow have been based on actual institutional, campus, and classroom situations. Some I experienced firsthand; many have come to my attention from colleagues across the nation. These scenarios (stories) provide a starting point for conversation with your colleagues. Regardless of the subject or topic of each scenario, you will find that they relate to the seven Rs for success—success for your students, and most importantly success for you and your colleagues.

• • •

It's time for a faculty resilience focus.

• • •

Of course, these scenarios represent a small fraction of the issues, challenges, and opportunities of teaching and learning. Each story can also be told from a number of perspectives. So, please keep in mind that this book is not meant to be an all-encompassing and thorough review of every issue in education. I'm not sure any book can do that. Where I do believe the strength of this book lies is in its facilitation of collegial conversations about the issues herein, which in turn, hopefully, will raise other issues particular to you and your institutional culture.

SCENARIO FORMAT

You will note that the scenarios are brief. Few exceed one page. They set the tone, establish a topic, introduce a dilemma, and present follow-up questions. Use the scenarios to connect with your campus and your professional experiences. Use them to tap into the collective wisdom of your colleagues. Brainstorm and pose specific strategic questions on how to resolve the issues presented.

For each scenario you will find

- The Title
  - Introduces the topic.
- An Organizing Question
  - Think of this as a lesson organizer.

- Video Introduction to the Scenario (by your author)
  - These will be brief (about sixty seconds).
- The scenario
  - The actual teaching and learning situation will be presented in a story format.
- Reflect on This
  - A few follow-up questions allow you to dig a bit deeper into the scenario topic. While each question can encourage great conversation, please do not feel obligated (or overwhelmed) to respond to all questions. Pick and choose as to what fits your particular needs on campus. Regardless of the scenario topic, consider using the following four questions to guide your conversation and thought processes:
    - What VISION do you have for this particular topic?
    - What specific CHALLENGES exist regarding this topic?
    - What ACTION will you take to address the challenges and move toward your vision?
    - What RESOURCES will you need?
- Consider This
  - Here you will find thoughts from the author (and literature) about the scenario topic.
- Applying the seven Rs
  - Before you move on to the next scenario, you will have the opportunity to apply the seven Rs. What connection(s) can you make between the material presented in this scenario and each of the seven Rs?

SCENARIO ORDER

In every book I have written, the Contents page always presented a dilemma. What should go first, appear in the middle, or end the work? If you ask ten people for their opinions, you will likely get ten different orders.

So, what you find in the Contents for this book represents my vision of how to order the scenarios. More specifically, what you find here is my vision of the order on the day I sent this to publication. It is not perfect. And, as in so many things in life, one scenario can very easily cross several lines of concern. That was a reason for me, including three versions of the Contents (sequential, categorical, and chronological).

Don't feel constrained by the order. Start wherever you believe works best for you, your colleagues, your students, and your campus.

Jargon-free Writing (I Hope!)

As I wrote this book, I did my best to remain jargon-free. I want the book to be approachable. It should not be a reading chore that requires constant referral to the dictionary.

One term does deserve note. Throughout the scenarios you will note that I often use the term "professor." At times I use "instructor" or "teacher" (which I prefer). Different institutions use different labels. Some institutions also use "associate professor." Regardless of the title, the focus herein remains on faculty resilience and growth.

Nothing Fancy

Read. Reflect. Respond.

That's it. I do not want you to get lost in endless pages of pontification. As stated above, I want to provide the framework for growth and resilience—and then step out of your way. This allows you the opportunity to have a conversation, explore, question, and learn.

Stay curious, my friend!

Steve Piscitelli
Atlantic Beach, Florida
2017

We Teach Much More Than Our Disciplines[3]

• • •

Organizing Question: What important questions should you be asking yourself as you plan a lesson, a unit, and a semester?

Go to www.stevepiscitelli.com for supporting video.

MORE THAN TWO DECADES AGO, a teaching and learning colleague passed along a lasting nugget of wisdom. On that particular day, we shared some of the daily struggles and challenges our students faced. While we both worked with students who lacked basic academic skills, all of our students had nonacademic challenges that presented obstacles to their academic progress. These included homelessness, domestic violence, substance abuse issues, financial challenges, childcare concerns, physical and cognitive disabilities, incarceration, and chronic health concerns. They brought powerful and far-ranging personal stories into the classroom each day.

My colleague simply stated, "Steve, we teach so much more than math or history or English or science."

Amen.

Over my more than three decades in the classroom, both teaching and learning have undergone a shift. Some even might say we have encountered a seismic transformation. When I look back to my experiences as an undergraduate student in the early 1970s, college teaching was for the most part about content-driven lectures. Today, we have come to focus more upon the interplay of academic and nonacademic issues that have an impact on the teaching and learning dynamic. Think of the craft of teaching like a dance. Those of us involved in the choreography need to pay attention to the rhythms, the tempo shifts, and who is on the dance floor.

Effective teachers provide engaging opportunities for students to discover that their studies have purpose beyond the classroom and that their individual efforts affect their successes. They, also, pay close attention to the seven Rs. These seven interrelated areas for personal development—relationships, relevance, rainbows, resources, responsibility, reflection, and resilience—drive classroom and life success.[4]

As you think about your students and plan your classes, consider each of the following:

* **Relationships**. Technology allows our students (and us) to have "friends" we have never met—and many of whom we probably never will or care to encounter. We need to help our students develop the skills of personal connections—meaningful connections and networks for a greater purpose. How do you help your students focus on building supportive networks?
    * **Consider This**. Begin face-to-face (or online) relationship building the first day of class, if not before.[5] In addition to whatever community-building exercises you use to help students get to know one another, consider what you will share about *your journey* in higher education or life in general. Being mindful of your boundaries and limits with what you share, this personal introduction can go a long way in setting the tone for the class and the semester. Think of your most influential teachers from your past. What did they do to build relationships in the classroom? Why do you think they had success doing this?

- **Relevance**. Demonstrate to students that their learning in the classroom has relevance to their lives outside of class and to their future careers. Help them understand that what you are teaching (the content) is more than arcane and isolated pieces of data. If student's can see the relevance of what you present, that's inspirational! Einstein reportedly said that "Education is not the learning of facts. It's rather the training of the mind to think." What innovative methods have you used to make your classes consistently relevant and to encourage your students to think?
  - **Consider This**. I made a promise to my students the first day of each semester: "If, at the end of a class session, you cannot apply what you read for class and/or what we discussed in class to your life outside of the classroom, then I failed you that day." So, whether I delivered a lesson on the catalysts for the Declaration of Independence or the application of test-taking strategies, I always worked to make relevant connections to their lives beyond campus. Bring in current events, campus issues, and/or topics specific to your course content. If you have difficulty identifying the relevance, more than likely your students will as well. What adjustments can you make? Who can help you?
- **Rainbows**. Every student comes to campus with dreams. Some arrive laser-focused; others come a bit confused. And, still other students will switch their majors. When students can see their own brightly colored rainbows, then their own purpose comes into clearer focus (just like for you and me) and their campus experiences have more relevance (see above). That's inspirational! How do you help your students focus on their rainbows—articulate their dreams—and take specific steps to move toward those dreams?
  - **Consider This**. Even the best students need a little cheerleading at times. They need a reminder not to give up on their

rainbows. I found regular reflective assignments, that allowed them to make connections between their college work and their dreams, to be effective (see Relevance above). In addition, I found that a targeted email (about four weeks from the *end* of the semester) reminding them to stay connected (or reconnect) to their long-term goals worked as a booster shot for their energy.[6] "Now is your time," I would tell them, "to make those dreams come true, to seek Resources (see below) that can help you reach your dreams, and to strengthen Relationships (see above) for support and direction." What can you do to help your students stay on track and focus on their dreams?

* **Resources.** Think of the times you may have struggled in your chosen calling. Even the seasoned songwriter and author hits the wall and comes up dry from time to time. The prolific salesperson experiences a slump. And the straight-A student will sure enough run into his or her toughest professor ever! Your students probably will never be in another place in their lives, like your institution, with so many resources dedicated to their success. How do you help your students learn about the resources, find them, and use them?

   * **Consider This.** Help your students find key resources with my "3-in-15" approach. For instance, ask various student affairs colleagues (financial aid, career center, and registration for example) to come to your class and share the *three* most important Resources available in their area for student and life success. And limit their presentation to *fifteen* minutes. This helps to focus student attention as well as the guest speaker's presentation. Don't firehouse your students with an endless list of resources they "might need" at some point. Focus on key ones they need at a certain point in the term. As an added bonus, once the presentation is completed and the students have asked questions, consider a "field trip" to that resource's part of the campus. Then the

students will have (1) heard about the resource, (2) discussed the resource, and (3) visited the resource. What effective strategy do you use or can you use to help your students "collide with resources"?

• • •

Seven interrelated areas for personal development drive classroom and life success.

• • •

◆ **Responsibility.** I have met a lot of people with ambition. I have worked with individuals who had potential. But I have found that without initiative, the first two will not amount to much. All three are needed: the desire (ambition), the ability (potential), *and* the drive (initiative). The sweet spot is the intersection of all three. This takes discipline (and the influence of the other six principles). You and your colleagues can craft magnificent lessons and provide spot-on resources, but if the students do not do their part, they will not succeed. Like a personal trainer at the gym, you show them techniques and tools. They, however, must do the heavy lifting. They need the grit and Resilience (see below) to persevere. How can you help your students clearly identify what they need to do and how they need to do?

  ◆ **Consider This.** Just like fuel alone in the gas tank won't get us to a destination, hope without action will not get any of us to our Rainbows (see above). We must step on the gas pedal. *Hope* needs to be combined with *Planning* and *Action* in order to get to the *Destination* (H + P + A = D.) Encourage your students to identify the "nonnegotiable" parts of their lives. These represent the priority items and actions that will help them move toward their dreams. They should also identify their "negotiables" that have become distractions on the way to their destination. The best place to start this is with an accurate log of how they use their 168 weekly hours. Until any of us know how we use our Resources (time, for instance), it is difficult to understand where we need to make adjustments. How do you or can you help your students clarify what they need to do and how they need to do it?

• **Reflection.** When I think back on my early years of teaching, when I was developing my "teaching chops," I shudder a bit. I stood in front of the room and did lots of talking. My training and modeling, for the most part, had come from lecturing teachers and professors. I had content to deliver, and lecture seemed to be the most efficient means. That my students did well was, I believe, a testament to their resilience in the face of this nonstop firehose of information. Over the years, I adjusted my approach by bringing in more collaborative activities and more time for my students to reflect on what was being tossed at them. I developed provocative questions for oral discussions and written responses. As much as the "what" of their education is important, our students need time to reflect on the "why" of what they are doing and (hopefully) learning. This awareness helps to create Relevance (see above) and create a sense of where they stand in this world (see Relationships, above). Reflection develops and fine-tunes personal stories. Such awareness takes practice to develop. Do we give students time to truly reflect on what they are doing in class and in their lives?

  • **Consider This.** Have the students draw a line down the center of a piece of paper. At the top of the left column, let them write the word "VALUE," and at the top of the right column, write the word "TIME." In the VALUE column, ask them to list three things that are the most valuable/the biggest priorities in their lives right now. These are their non-negotiables. In the TIME column, they list the three things that take most of their time each week. The final step can be an eye-opener. When they look at what they *say* they value and how they *actually* use their time, do they see any disconnections? The value column represents the stories they tell themselves. The time column represents the stories they live.[7] In his book *The Little Book of Talent*, Daniel Coyle challenges his readers to "Stare at who you want to become."[8] Go a step further and ask your students to "Stare at who you have become on the way to becoming who you want to become!" None of us are completed projects. We have the opportunity to continue to evolve until we stop breathing. How do you help your students sort through and continue to write and live their stories?

* **Resilience.** We live multidimensional lives, and so do our students. We are not "just a student" or "just a teacher" or "just a [you fill in the blank]." If we don't take care of ourselves, if we don't maintain a sense of balance, how will we be able to reach our goals (see Rainbows, above)? While labels might differ, we essentially have six dimensions to our lives: social, occupational, spiritual, physical, intellectual, and emotional.[9] We have to keep them tuned and balanced. When one dimension (say, emotional or physical or social) is out of tune, it will affect the others. This requires that we take Responsibility (see above) to make time for meaningful Reflection (see above). How do we help our students understand they need to maintain a healthy balance in their lives? How do we connect them to strategies to maintain balance and well-being? We have tutoring rooms. Do we have resilience rooms?

  * **Consider This.** It happens to all of us at one time or another. One of our life dimensions will get out of tune. When one or more of our life dimensions plays an off-note, that is the time to Hit The Reset Button (HTRB)[10]—to retune so we can play the beautiful music we have inside of us. Make well-being a nonnegotiable emphasis on your campus. Help students become more attuned to their energy levels. That includes

diet, exercise, and proper sleep. Guest speakers, workshops, quick-hit articles in the campus newspaper, and posts on social media can keep well-being in the forefront. Relationships and Resources can help (see above) as well. How does your course, your program, and your institution help students build resilience?

Success is the product of small yet consistent choices we all make and do (or don't do) each day. The seven Rs —when understood and faithfully applied—can help our students stay the course, continue their journey, and enjoy growth and resilience.

Yes, we do teach much more than our disciplines.

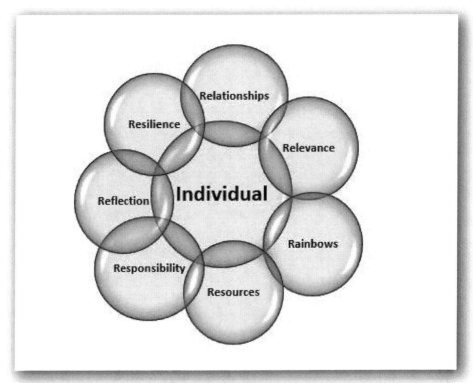

The Seven Rs for Success

YOUR CAMPUS ALL-STARS!

Every department, every program, and every college or university I visit has its own homegrown all-stars. Often they quietly go about their teaching, seldom calling attention to themselves. Do yourself a favor and seek out these colleagues. Even if they do not want the "spotlight," ask if you can have lunch with them, shadow them, observe one of their class sessions, or bounce an idea off them you may have for your classes. Don't rely solely on outside experts to tell you about powerful teaching and learning strategies. You have treasures on your campus. Find these resources and tap into their wisdom!

The following activity can help you focus on these inspiring colleagues.

THE SEVEN RS IN ACTION: YOUR COLLEAGUES AS INSPIRATION!

Think of your colleagues for a moment. Think of what they do in their teaching and learning practices that inspires you. List three of those practices below—three inspiring teaching and learning practices that hold promise for making a difference in the lives of students. Also, to which principle(s) of success (the seven Rs) do these practices connect?

1. Inspiring Practice 1: _____
   _____

   a. In what ways do you find this practice to be inspiring?_____
      _____

   b. This practice connects to R_____
      _____

2. Inspiring Practice 2:_____
   _____

   a. In what ways do you find this practice to be inspiring?_____
      _____

    b. This practice connects to R_____

_____

3. Inspiring Practice 3: _____

_____

    a. In what ways do you find this practice to be inspiring?_____

_____

    b. This practice connects to R_____

_____

THE SEVEN RS IN ACTION: YOU AS INSPIRATION!

Think of your teaching experience for a moment.[†] Consider those practices—classroom activities, discussions, presentations, and the like—that *you* have done that have inspired your students or colleagues. List three of those practices below—three inspiring teaching and learning practices that hold promise for making a difference in the lives of students and in the lives of your colleagues. Also, to which principle(s) of success (the seven Rs) do these practices connect?

1. Inspiring Practice 1: _____

_____

    a. In what ways do you find this practice to be inspiring?_____

_____

    b. This practice connects to R_____

_____

2. Inspiring Practice 2: _____

_____

---

† If you are a first-year instructor, consider times when you led study groups, or made a class presentation, or performed in front of an audience.

    a. In what ways do you find this practice to be inspiring?_____

    _____

    b. This practice connects to R_____

    _____

3. Inspiring Practice 3:_____

    _____

    a. In what ways do you find this practice to be inspiring?_____

    _____

    b. This practice connects to R_____

    _____

APPLYING THE SEVEN RS: THE REST OF THIS BOOK

The remainder of this book will use the seven Rs as a foundation for teaching and learning. You will be asked how you do or how you can incorporate these principles into your work with students. You will be encouraged to connect these principles to your life and relationships beyond the classroom—just like you want your students to do. Again, draw on the collective genius of your colleagues.

Read. Reflect. Respond.

What Is Your Story?

• • •

Organizing Question: In what ways can your story be inspirational for your students?

Go to www.stevepiscitelli.com for supporting video.

The Story of the Lavender Farmer[11]

Robin worked in the business world for thirteen years. She served as an administrative assistant; she loved her job. Then came the downsizing. Her boss offered her one day less of work for half the pay—in other words, work 80 percent of what she used to but for 50 percent of the pay. She opted for a buyout and, then, she and her husband, Chris, considered their next move on their journey ahead.

As often happens, a chance encounter can present options we never knew of or considered before. Such was the situation when Robin paid a visit to a friend's home to help her with some farm work. A little weeding and tending to a crop. Nothing too strenuous. Time with a friend.

That day, Robin worked some acreage devoted to a lavender crop. She liked the smell, the feel, and the work itself. As she talked with and worked beside her friend, Robin began constructing a story: What if I grew lavender? Why not me?

She had no background in this. She had no land to plant the crop. And she and her husband did not have a great deal of money to invest. She did have her company severance, but that was pretty much spoken for with bills and other commitments.

After talking and planning, she and Chris were able to sublet a small plot of her in-laws' farm. Her lavender dream was moving closer to reality.

They bought two hundred young lavender plants and began their venture. Two years and two harvests later, Robin and her husband started working on the next phase—the manufacturing of the lavender into products like sachet and soap.

As she told me about this next step, her eyes widened and her voice brightened beyond her already pleasant demeanor. You could tell this venture clearly ignited her passion. Small steps leading to personal satisfaction.

They, also, had a small plot of land in Idaho, she told me. They decided to see how that land and lavender would work together. Robin and her husband planted two crops of seedlings—and, unfortunately, each year the seedlings vanished! They never knew exactly what happened. A slight detour on the way to their dream.

An additional challenge came that second year when wildfires torched their land. Through it all, though, Robin and her husband maintained a resilient attitude.

"It has been a saga, but I am determined to be successful, and continue to learn from each chapter," she said. "Thank goodness they come one at a time."

I wrote those words toward the end of 2015. And each time I reread them, I get energized. People like Robin and Chris remind us of the power of considered thought and action. While they were moving into new territory (metaphorically and literally), they did not let the newness (for them) of the venture dissuade them. They prepared themselves to take risks, to take action, and they did not let "perfect" stand in the way of movement. Failure was an option. And so was fulfillment and excitement. They could have stood on the other side of the fence dreaming of lavender—and never have done anything out of fear of disappointment. That would have, more than likely, led to a lot of "what ifs" in the future.

Thanks to Robin, Chris, and their lavender crop for reminding us that meaningful growth generally does not come to the timid let's-fly-under-the-radar person. And it does not come in one fell swoop as manna dropping from the skies. It takes work, preparation, faith, and resilience. Yes, there more than likely will be a disappointing chapter or two or more along the way. This reminds us of the importance of resilience.

So, I'd like for you to push your modesty to the side for a few minutes. Think of your story—your journey to the classroom as a teacher. Think of the challenges (and maybe even hardships) you encountered, experienced, and endured. Think of your mistakes, miscues, and meanderings. And think of all your accomplishments, achievements, and attainments.

YOUR STORY may very well show someone the light in a time of darkness or despair. YOUR STORY needs to be heard. YOUR STORY, the blemishes and the successes, can be inspirational for others and a reminder to yourself. In those times when you feel a bit down or totally despondent, perhaps a look back on what you have accomplished will help reignite the spark and rekindle your spirit. Take a moment and complete the following exercise. As you reflect on your responses, consider using the following four questions to guide your thoughts.

* What VISION do you have for this particular story and how to relate it?
* What specific CHALLENGES exist regarding the sharing of your story?
* What ACTION will you take to address the challenges and move toward your vision?
* What RESOURCES will you need?

Your Story

Your autobiography may well contain instructive stories from which your students can learn. Perhaps you were a first-generation student. Maybe you had to attend school part time as you earned money to pay tuition. Did you confront learning challenges and/or physical disabilities? Use the space below to list three challenges you have overcome and/or achievements you savored that could be inspirational for your students.[†]

[†] One note of caution: Always be sure to maintain appropriate professional boundaries and limits. Remember, our students are not our therapy groups!

1.
2.
3.

In what ways do you think your story can help you connect with and guide your students? What lessons are present?

CONSIDER THIS

YOUR STORY, the successes as well as the stumbles, can be inspirational. Every faculty member who stands before a class of students has a story to share. It doesn't have to be the stuff that makes a melodrama. It does not have to be one that brought you back from the brink of utter disaster and failure. And your story does not need to be "sexy." It needs to be authentic. And who is a more authentic YOU than YOU?

A number of years ago, someone told me that my story did not resonate. I was told that no one really wanted to hear about how I was a successful student or how I earned the distinction of being my college class valedictorian. Audiences would more readily connect with the stories of the "bad" student who made "good." My story, was just not compelling or sexy enough.

I thought then and still think now that my consistent and disciplined good habits in school and life can be (and have been) inspirational. Maybe the mistakes or missteps I made were not cataclysmic enough to draw gasps from people preconditioned for "reality and survivor stories." My experiences still, though, helped me persevere and build resilience. And I believed (accurately as it turned out) that they could be instructive for students and colleagues as well.

• • •

Think of your story—your journey to the class-room as a teacher. It can be inspirational.

• • •

Applying The Seven Rs

Before you move on to the next scenario, revisit the seven Rs. What connection(s) can you make between the material presented in this scenario and each of the seven Rs? Once you have completed that, star the principle (the one "R") that seems to be the most significant in this context and reflect on why you believe this is the most significant principle.

- Relationships
- Relevance
- Rainbows
- Resources
- Responsibility
- Reflection
- Resilience

I Am, Therefore I Profess!

• • •

Organizing Question: When you consider what you do in your classroom each day of the semester, how do you know you are relevant?

Go to www.stevepiscitelli.com for supporting video.

PROFESSOR DESCARTES HAD JUST LEFT the semester's kick-off faculty convocation. He was not happy. As he walked to his campus office, he stopped by a colleague's office to blow off some steam.

"Just another typical talking head with nothing useful to say," said Descartes about the morning speaker. "Did you hear that drivel about relevance in the classroom? Are you kidding me! Our students need discipline. I don't have time—and frankly, they don't need for me to take the time—to talk about current events and life 'out there.' Even the curriculum the administration expects us to follow is impractical. I know what the students need to be successful. Pure and simple, I am a professor. Therefore, my job is to profess! Their job is to take notes and follow what I say. End of discussion. Relevance? Bah!"

REFLECT ON THIS

- What are your thoughts about Professor Descartes's complaints?
- Is a professor's job merely to "profess"?

* Can a classroom be "disciplined" and relevant to life "out there"? If so, in what ways?
* Is the principle of "relevance" relevant in any classroom? Why or why not?
* What impact can professors have on the curriculum they have for their courses?
* Complete the following four-part exercise by thinking of the students who cross the threshold of your classroom each semester.

As you consider the specific reflection steps above, you may wish to give broader thought to the following:

* What VISION do you have regarding teaching and relevance?
* What specific CHALLENGES exist regarding this topic?
* What ACTION will you take to address the challenges and move toward your vision?
* What RESOURCES will you need?

Consider This

Rather than tell our students how important our class, course, or program will be to them, we would do better to demonstrate how relevant the class, course, or program is to their lives. In short, does your time with the students make a difference to them?[12]

In her book *Meaningful: The Story of Ideas That Fly*, Bernadette Jiwa drives home the point that we need to "start the innovation journey with the customer's story and allow our customers to become not just our target, but our muse."[13]

Consider her words when you think about your students.‡

---

‡ The word "customer" can be a hot-button word for some in higher education. Jiwa was not writing about schools; she was addressing businesses and entrepreneurs. Don't get lost in that. The point remains: How do you start your journey of connection with your students? How do you and the course material remain relevant?

The first day of the semester (in my student-success classes) I started with my students sharing their dreams with the class. Their dreams became a running theme in the class.§ It made the class more relevant to them. Yes, there was a course outline and the textbook—but the approach to the material had to resonate with and connect to the people in front of me. I had to attempt to understand their story rather than force-feed them my story. Yes, my story could be instructive (see Scenario 1, above)—but it certainly was not the main focus of this play. I attempted to tap into their feelings and emotions by using reflective exercises that helped them connect chapter concepts to their dreams. To them college was not simply about a degree. It was about a better life for them and their families.

One example: As a way to understand the critical thinking model we used in class, the students applied the three steps directly to their dreams.[14] First, they had to identify assumptions they were making about why they wanted "to do" what they wanted to do for a career. This eventually led to discussions about earnings, lifestyle, and community standing. Then I encouraged them to evaluate the information they had about their career (or major)—and start listing questions about what they did not know. This brought them to a third step, asking them to draw conclusions about their chosen career path based on where they were in the process right now. From there they could clarify their goal(s) and take specific steps needed. At the very least, this process gave them something concrete and personal with which to apply an abstract critical thinking model.

Another example: My history students received my promise that each day they would be able to apply the assigned readings and class discussions to their lives beyond campus. For instance, each day I brought in a current event to emphasize the historical period we were studying. Or when we discussed the origins of the political party system, we examined labels and what parties stood for in different eras of history. They made observations about what was different today. When they read documents like the Declaration of Independence, I asked them whether it was a "live" document or not.

§ The theme of my student-success classes focused on two questions: (1) What is your dream? (2) What are you doing to move toward your dream?

That is, based on the argument presented in 1776 for independence, could a state or region declare independence today? That generally brought about considerable discussion. And it got them excited about history (OK, not all of them—but many!). To be certain, the students had responsibilities in this dance; they needed to pay attention to guidance provided. They had to follow through on assignments and be engaged in class. Of course, this also meant the assignments and classwork I orchestrated had to have relevance. [**] As Jiwa pointedly proves with various case studies, "The best way to get attention is to give it unconditionally first."

Relevance. Content. Meaning. Connection.

Here is a personal reflective exercise you can do to reinforce the idea of relevance.

BEFORE

It's the first day of the semester. If you had to write a composite of what your students bring to the classroom, what would that story include? Think of attitudes, financial situations, family stability, health, relationships with authority figures, relationship building skills, punctuality, dependability, civility, knowledge about their skillsets, connection to campus resources, connection to technology, and collaboration skills. Be as specific as you can be.

AFTER

It is the end of the semester. If you had to write a composite of your students' lives at the end of the semester, what would that story include? What changes or tweaks have they made in areas such as financial situations, family stability, health, relationships with authority figures, relationship building, punctuality, dependability, civility, knowledge about their skillsets, connection to campus

---

[**] You might note three of the seven Rs here: Relevance, Reflection, and Responsibility.

resources, connection to technology, and collaboration skills? Be as specific as you can be.

BECAUSE

What changes occurred for your students because of your class, course, or personal connections? In short, how relevant was your time with your students to their lives?

EVIDENCE

How do you know what you say above is accurate?

• • •

Does your time with the students make a difference to them?

• • •

Applying The Seven Rs
Before you move on to the next scenario, revisit the seven Rs. What connection(s) can you make between the material presented in this scenario and each of the seven Rs? Once you have completed that, star the principle (the one "R") that seems to be the most significant in this context and reflect on why you believe this is the most significant principle.

* Relationships
* Relevance
* Rainbows
* Resources
* Responsibility
* Reflection
* Resilience

What Do You Want to Talk About?††

• • •

Organizing Question: What can an instructor do to inspire students who demonstrate a lack of enthusiasm and interest in the subject matter and class activities?

Go to www.stevepiscitelli.com for supporting video.

PROFESSOR KEATS TEACHES A LITERATURE class. His passion is poetry. He recognizes that his students may not find poetry as energizing as he does. So, he attempts, as much as possible, to start class conversations about current events and pop culture that relate to his course's concepts. He brings in politics, music, movies, and sports among other topics. When he puts a question to the class, the students respond with complete silence. At most, one or two students may respond, kind of perfunctorily.

Even when tying questions to fields of study like Journalism or Music, there is no enthusiasm.

He typically resorts to "What do you want to talk about?" Again, nothing from the students.

Keats has come to you, a wise mentor and veteran teacher in the department, and asks, "Is the apathy a result of the subject/discipline? Is the current generation *that* tuned out about the world around them? How can I generate some life and relevance in the classroom and the subject matter?"

---

†† Thanks to my colleague professor Matt Mitchell of Florida State College at Jacksonville for the inspiration for this scenario.

Reflect on This

- Should Professor Keats even worry about injecting relevance into a literature class?
- Suggest three strategies that Professor Keats can attempt with his class to help move them from disinterest to, at least, more engagement.
- What do you believe accounts for reactions (or lack of reactions) such as those described in this scenario?
- Is the professor asking the correct questions in class to establish connections?

As you consider the specific reflection questions above, you may wish to give broader thought to the following:

- What VISION do you have regarding teaching, relevance, and student engagement?
- What specific CHALLENGES exist regarding this topic?
- What ACTION will you take to address the challenges and move toward your vision?
- What RESOURCES will you need?

Consider This

Finding relevance to class material can be challenging at times. But as pointed out in other scenarios of this book, if you are not relevant for your students, then why are they in this class?

You can address relevance on a number of levels.

- At a most basic level, the significance of the class can simply be that students must progress through it to get to the next level of studies. A general education/core requirement class could fit this description. However, even this must go beyond the admonishment: "This class is important because you need to pass it!"

* What connections can you show the students between the class material and their majors? For instance, I once had a student who wanted to be a nurse. She questioned why she needed to write essays. Her job, according to her assumptions, would not require that kind of communication.

   This led to a class discussion about how essay writing honed the ability to accurately describe events and/or their consequences. We then looked at how that could be practical for a nurse.

   I then took the students to a website that posted job listings. When we looked at the necessary skills for a nurse, we found that effective "oral and written communication" were required. At the least, this can provide a conversation starter about the importance of communication.

* Some classes such as history and political science can find relevance in the day's news.

* Math classes can examine community architecture or road projects. How is math critical to these projects? After all, would you want to drive across a bridge whose engineers had made mathematical errors in the final project?

* English classes can review websites or the community newspaper for errors and, as well, for expertly written pieces.

What has worked in your area?

• • •

Finding relevance to class material
can be challenging at times.

• • •

APPLYING THE SEVEN RS

Before you move on to the next scenario, revisit the seven Rs. What connection(s) can you make between the material presented in this scenario and each of the seven Rs? Once you have completed that, star the principle (the one "R") that seems to be the most significant in this context and reflect on why you believe this is the most significant principle.

* Relationships
* Relevance
* Rainbows
* Resources
* Responsibility
* Reflection
* Resilience

The First Day of Class

• • •

Organizing Question: How do you know what you do on the first day of class is effective?

Go to www.stevepiscitelli.com for supporting video.

INSTRUCTOR FIBONACCI APPROACHES THE DOOR of his classroom. "Hmm," he thinks to himself. "This doesn't bode well. Class starts in two minutes, and only three students are waiting to enter the room. The roll says I have twenty-five on the list."

As he approaches the door, the three students have their gazes buried in their respective cell phones. No one speaks to anyone. Professor Fibonacci quietly unlocks the door, and the students follow him into the room.

"I assume the rest of your classmates are looking for nonexistent parking spots. I will wait an extra ten minutes before I start class today." No one acknowledges the professor, so he busies himself turning on the computer and projector. He quietly excuses himself and returns to his office across the hall to gather up the handouts for the day: class syllabus, class handout packet, homework assignment for the first night, and a list of important contact numbers on campus. He looks around and spies an empty box in the office corner, piles the packets into it, and lugs it across the hall. Five minutes have elapsed.

When he returns to the classroom, he finds a little more activity and energy. Fifteen of the twenty-five students have shown up and found seats.

Professor Fibonacci drops the box on his desk and proceeds to place a syllabus and handout packet in front of each student.

When he completes the distribution, he notes that it's ten past the hour, so he begins his lecture.

Standing behind his desk, he begins: "Good morning, class. I'm Professor Fibonacci. I have been teaching for twenty-five years. Welcome to math. You have your syllabus in front of you. You're in college, so you don't need me to read this to you. It's your responsibility to know what is there. We have a great deal to cover, so let's get right to it. Don't want to waste any of your tuition money!"

He smiles at what he considers a witticism. The students barely notice. Some still are texting. Others have leaned back in their chairs with blank stares cast in the professor's general direction. A handful of students take paper from their backpacks and begin to take notes.

"Math is tough—and it is relevant to your lives. For instance, look at the board and you will see a sequence of numbers. There is a pattern. Can you see it? You *can* see it, can't you?"

Not one student responds. One actually seems to be sleeping in the back of the room.

"Well, before we get to that," the professor continues, undeterred by what he considers a typical lack of enthusiasm by typically unmotivated students, "please clear your desks." He waves a stack of papers in his hand toward the direction of the students.

"This is a diagnostic test. The results will let me know who really belongs in this class and who will have difficulties. You will have forty-five minutes to complete it. No calculators will be allowed. Best wishes!"

And with that, Professor Fibonacci starts his twenty-sixth year of teaching.

REFLECT ON THIS

* Consider what and how Professor Fibonacci did what he did. If you had to give him collegial feedback, what would you say about the following?
    * What did he do particularly well?
    * The time he arrived to the classroom?
    * Going back to his office to retrieve class materials?
    * His method of syllabus distribution?
    * His decision to start class ten minutes late?
    * Not taking class attendance?
    * Jumping right into the class material?
    * Texting in the classroom?
    * Anything else he could have done better?
* Extra Credit! ☺
    * Rewrite the scenario and have Professor Fibonacci do what you would envision a master teacher would do in this situation.

As you consider the specific reflection questions above, you may wish to give broader thought to the following:

* What VISION do you have regarding the atmosphere, tone, and expectations you establish the first day of class?
* What specific CHALLENGES exist regarding the first day of class?
* What ACTION will you take to address the challenges and move toward your vision?
* What RESOURCES will you need?

CONSIDER THIS

The first day of class is arguably the most important day of the school term. This is when impressions are made and connections have either begun or been dashed. As the teacher, think to a time when you entered a room of strangers. It could've been a party. Maybe it was your first day on campus as a teacher. Do you remember how you felt? Perhaps you were excited with a tinge of anxiety. Or maybe you experienced symptoms of full-blown fear and wanted to run away.

Our students can feel the same range of emotions.

Also, think of teachers from your past who made a powerful impression on your first day in their class. What did they do?

At times we may get caught up in checking off boxes for all the *things* we need the first day.

* Do I have my syllabus? ✓
* Do I have my room keys? ✓
* Do I have the class attendance list? ✓
* Do I have handouts, supplements, and textbooks? ✓

All these remain important (and our professor in the scenario above may have fallen short on a few). But there are so many other questions to consider. [15] You will find an exhaustive list of twenty-five categories of questions in Appendix A. Pick and choose which questions work best for you. Use them as conversation starters. Perhaps a few will rise to the level of the "Top Ten Questions" every faculty member needs to ask before going into the first day of class. Continue to be curious—and continue to grow.

• • •

Think of teachers from your past who made a power-
ful impression on your first day in their class.

• • •

Applying The Seven Rs

Before you move on to the next scenario, revisit the seven Rs. What connection(s) can you make between the material presented in this scenario and each of the seven Rs? Once you have completed that, star the principle (the one "R") that seems to be the most significant in this context and reflect on why you believe this is the most significant principle.

- Relationships
- Relevance
- Rainbows
- Resources
- Responsibility
- Reflection
- Resilience

SCENARIO 5

They Just Copied and Pasted

• • •

Organizing Question: What can instructors do when their students do not understand (or adhere to) the basic expectations of information literacy?

Go to www.stevepiscitelli.com for supporting video.

PROFESSOR HOFFMAN HAS BEEN TEACHING introduction to literature for years. Over that time, he has fine-tuned his syllabus, gathered a notebook full of examples, and has a PowerPoint slide deck for each unit he teaches. He also has gathered a number of YouTube videos that address his favorite pieces of literature.

It is now the third week of the term. Today, Professor Hoffman received his students' first drafts of their term research paper. He was appalled to say the least. During lunch with you, he laid out the problems.

"My students have great difficulty working with source material and incorporating it into a paper. They can find sources easily enough, but they have trouble with really understanding what they read. So, they don't paraphrase or summarize the information well. Heck, most times I found they just copied and pasted!" He shook his head in disbelief.

He continued, "They often miss the point altogether, or misinterpret what they think they've read. If we read any essays that are slightly above average in difficulty, many just give up and would rather fail a quiz or not submit homework than wrestle with it. Where's their gumption? They are very passive readers—which often carries over to being passive learners as well."

He took a sip from his water bottle and thought for a moment. "I have all this information I prepared for the semester, but they don't understand the basic stuff. I don't know how they'll pass the course—any of them!" He looked at you and asked, "What would you do?[‡‡]

REFLECT ON THIS

* You are Professor Hoffman's colleague. How would you approach the situation with the students?
* At first blush, it appears the students do not understand (or ignore) basic rules regarding citations. Do you detect any other concerns or challenges for both the students and the professor in this scenario?
* Reread Professor Hoffman's concerns, and list three major challenges his students face based on his experiences. Can you connect any of these to your experiences with your students?
* How would you specifically handle each of the three challenges you have listed?

As you consider the specific reflection questions above, you may wish to give broader thought to the following:

* What VISION do you have regarding your students and information literacy?
* What specific CHALLENGES exist regarding this topic?
* What ACTION will you take to address the challenges and move toward your vision?
* What RESOURCES will you need?

[‡‡] Thanks to my colleague professor Nancy Bullard of Florida State College at Jacksonville for the inspiration for this scenario.

CONSIDER THIS

We have a dilemma. The Internet has allowed us to access a dizzying array of information with the click of a mouse at our computer or the swipe of a finger on our tablet.[16] That's great! No matter the topic or challenge we may have in front of us, we can quickly find hundreds or thousands or hundreds of thousands of links to information. And that is what is not so great. With so much information, how do we know—and how do we help our students understand—how to separate the accurate from the suspect? Not all information is created equally.[17]

Perhaps you have the expectation that students should know how to find and use appropriate information for an assignment. Consider this question: How often is that expectation met by your students at a consistently high level of efficacy?

Think of your course—your discipline—and strategize with a colleague how to best help your students answer the following four questions about a specific assignment.

* What information do they need to complete the assignment? This requires that students understand the assignment, the vocabulary, and the expectations. What can you do—beyond just telling them—to help them understand this critical first step?
* Where can they find the information (sources) that will best help them complete the assignment appropriately and effectively? Perhaps your campus reference librarian can help students navigate the physical stacks of books in the media center as well as the millions of potential hits on the Internet.
* What standards have you set up with your students to help them evaluate the quality and usefulness of the information they find? One source has found that 90 percent of users click on links that appear on the first page of a Google search. Only 5 percent bother with the second page. Getting a site on the first page of a search engine has become a strategy in itself. [18] Help your students to help themselves be critical thinkers about the information they

see (and don't see). Devise strategic examples that have relevance to their lives. For instance, engage them in a conversation about how they would go about evaluating information to buy a new cell phone, tablet, or laptop. Ask them how they could apply those same or similar strategies to evaluate sources they use for a class assignment.

* Once they have found and evaluated the information, do they know how to appropriately organize, use, and present the information? Perhaps a conversation about "knowing your audience" would help them. Review proper paraphrasing and citation format as well.

• • •

Not *all* information is created equally.

• • •

Applying The Seven Rs

Before you move on to the next scenario, revisit the seven Rs. What connection(s) can you make between the material presented in this scenario and each of the seven Rs? Once you have completed that, star the principle (the one "R") that seems to be the most significant in this context and reflect on why you believe this is the most significant principle.

* Relationships
* Relevance
* Rainbows
* Resources
* Responsibility
* Reflection
* Resilience

SCENARIO 6

I Don't Want to Burn Out

• • •

Organizing Question: How can you recognize warnings of stress and burnout—and what steps can you take to effectively address these issues?

Go to www.stevepiscitelli.com for supporting video.

PROFESSOR JOHNSON DECIDED TO CLEAR a space in her calendar to attend a series of on-campus reflective practice discussions.[19] Even though this is her first semester as a full-time faculty member, her faculty mentor suggested she consider this workshop. "It will provide you with strategies to become more aware of what and why you do what you do in the classroom."

At the initial meeting, the workshop facilitator asked the participants why they had signed up for these reflective practice sessions. Professor Johnson was prepared to jokingly say that her mentor made her do it—but as she listened to her more senior colleagues share their reasons, she came to a different and more sobering realization.

Of the nine faculty members participating in this workshop, two said they were present because they had burned out and had lost their passion for teaching. They hoped this might help rekindle their spirits. Four other colleagues said they were in the process of a slow burnout. They were experiencing difficulty connecting with their students as they once had done. They could sense they were losing patience with their students and colleagues. Each said it had become tougher to find meaning in their work.

Professor Johnson took in each of these genuine responses. When her turn came around, she simply stated, "I don't want to burn out. That is why I am here. I want to learn from you what to do and what *not* to do."

REFLECT ON THIS

- What causes burnout?
- Can burnout be avoided?
- If Professor Johnson came to you and asked you for strategies to avoid burnout, what would be your top two or three strategies?
- What resources are available at your institution to help faculty avoid or at least recognize burnout?

As you consider the specific reflection questions above, you may wish to give broader thought to the following:

- What VISION do you have regarding teaching, burnout, and resilience?
- What specific CHALLENGES exist regarding this topic?
- What ACTION will you take to address the challenges and move toward your vision?
- What RESOURCES will you need?

CONSIDER THIS

A 2012 study of undergraduate teaching faculty found that factors such as committee assignments, teaching load, bureaucratic expectations (paperwork), lack of life-work balance, and self-imposed high expectations contributed to stress and burnout.[20] Those faculty had an awareness of stressors. That is an important first step. But, like our professor in the above scenario, recognition can (and needs to) generate questions about why we find ourselves in such situations, and what we can do moving forward. Consider using the simple strategy of *The Three As*: Awareness, Assumptions, and Actions.[21]

- ♦ <u>Awareness.</u> Professor Johnson above said she wanted to learn "what to do and what not to do." The first step has to be one of awareness. How will you become aware of those situations and factors that can lead to your burnout? Who can help you? Consider this the WHAT of burnout. What are the precipitating factors in your life?
- ♦ <u>Assumptions.</u> Once you have a handle on the WHAT, it is time to examine the WHY behind the WHAT. Why do you believe the factors you identified above have the impact they do on your professional and personal life? Why do you do what you do? That is, why do you respond/react the way you do in classroom and collegial situations? Why do you believe you teach (pedagogically speaking) the way you do? What choices do you have and what choices do you make? In other words, engage in a strategic questioning session.[22] Start with one simple question: "What questions should I be asking myself about my actions and assumptions?" This is not an accusatorial exercise but rather clarifying reflection for you.
- ♦ <u>Actions.</u> Once you have a handle on the WHAT and WHY, it's time to consider the HOW. How will you work to control stress and strain? How will you not only survive but actually thrive in your calling and life beyond campus?[23] Can you describe (at the least, begin to describe) the vision you have for the manner in which you would like to live and work? This in turn leads to the identification of more WHATs and WHYs.

● ● ●

*How will you become aware of those situations
and factors that can lead to your burnout?*

● ● ●

Applying The Seven Rs

Before you move on to the next scenario, revisit the seven Rs. What connection(s) can you make between the material presented in this scenario and each of the seven Rs? Once you have completed that, star the principle (the one "R") that seems to be the most significant in this context and reflect on why you believe this is the most significant principle.

* Relationships
* Relevance
* Rainbows
* Resources
* Responsibility
* Reflection
* Resilience

Nothing Will Stand in My Way!

• • •

Organizing Question: How does your campus and institution connect faculty and students with the many resources available for their use?

Go www.stevepiscitelli.com for supporting video.

You TREASURE LOTTIE'S PRESENCE IN your classroom. In addition to being articulate, cheerful, and well-prepared, she is laser-focused on her dream of becoming a social worker. She stops by your office at least once a week for clarification or just to say hello. During those visits you have learned that Lottie is a first-generation college student who is not getting much support from home, either financially or emotionally. It has been, to say the least, a tough journey for her. Yet here she is about to finish her second college semester. Even though the semester has challenged her on many levels, she stands to earn a 3.2 GPA. She remains focused and wants to complete her course work as soon as possible. "I'm not going to let anything or anyone stand in the way of my dreams!" she said on more than one occasion.

Today, she entered your classroom about ten minutes late. This is highly unusual for her. You were distributing the final exam to the class. As she quietly took a seat in the back of the room, you noticed that she had several bruises on her neck and wrists. She appeared to be quietly crying. The other students glanced at her while you were distributing the exam. When you placed an exam in front of her, she quietly nodded her head but did not make eye contact with you.

Reflect on This

- What could you do if you were in such situations?
- If you were in the professor's place as noted in the scenario above, what is the first thing you believe you would need to do?
- What resources are available on your campus or elsewhere at your institution or in your community to help Lottie? That is, who will you work with on behalf of Lottie?
- What role and/or responsibilities will the professor have in assisting Lottie once she has been provided the resources to address her issue(s)?
- What type of training do you and/or your colleagues need to address this and similar issues? How will you advocate for this type of training?

As you consider the specific reflection questions above, you may wish to give broader thought to the following:

- What VISION do you have regarding how to recognize and address the nonacademic challenges your students bring to the classroom?
- What specific CHALLENGES exist regarding this topic?
- What ACTION will you take to address the challenges and move toward your vision?
- What RESOURCES will you need?

Consider This

Our students bring so much more than their academic skills and challenges to our classrooms.[24] The scenario above is a composite of numerous similar situations my students had. Over the last five years (2011–2015) of my tenure on campus, I had more frequent conversations with women students who had reported being recent victims of domestic violence. As most of my faculty colleagues, I was never trained to be a counselor or how to handle issues such as domestic violence.

My first concern in these encounters always focused on the immediate welfare and safety of the individual in front of me. Thankfully, I had developed a close working relationship with the student services counselors on my campus so that I could immediately connect a student with assistance. I would personally walk the student to the counselor's office so that immediate (formal) intervention could begin. The classwork, obviously, became a secondary concern at that moment.

This scenario highlights one of those many student challenge situations that focuses the spotlight on the need for a strong bridge between faculty and your student services colleagues. I learned early on that even though well-meaning, my execution in such situations could be less than satisfactory. That is where the appropriate mentoring by student services/affairs colleagues became critical for me and my students. If you don't have such collaboration on your campus, find a way to start the conversation. Who can be an advocate for building these bridges? Your dean? The counselors? You? When you know about institutional resources, you have a better chance of connecting your students to them.

• • •

Appropriate mentoring by counseling and advising colleagues became critical for me and my students.

• • •

Applying The Seven Rs

Before you move on to the next scenario, revisit the seven Rs. What connection(s) can you make between the material presented in this scenario and each of the seven Rs? Once you have completed that, star the

principle (the one "R") that seems to be the most significant in this context and reflect on why you believe this is the most significant principle.

- Relationships
- Relevance
- Rainbows
- Resources
- Responsibility
- Reflection
- Resilience

Classroom Crises

• • •

Organizing Question: Does your campus have a mechanism to help faculty effectively address and handle the various classroom crises that arise each semester?

Go to www.stevepiscitelli.com for supporting video.

ONE OF YOUR STUDENTS, JAKE, a middle-aged man, comes to your office after class and expresses that he feels "too stupid" to succeed in your course. It is the second week of the semester. He goes on to explain that he hoped school would change his life. He tells you that he recently was released from the hospital after an attempted suicide, just three weeks before starting classes.

"Well, my life has never really been in the right direction. Never really been too smart. Never really been too athletic. I never really had any talents. I just could not do anything with my life. No matter how hard I try, I'd just end up failing. About the only thing I ever did that was worthwhile was when I kicked the heroin habit with help from a twelve-step program. When I found this school, I thought it was going to change my life, turn everything around for me. But then when I started getting into the classes, I realized nothing changed. I am still the same failure I always was and always will be. This was my last chance in reforming my life."

He looks at you, shakes his head, and continues, "Since it wasn't successful, I thought I might as well..."

He stops midsentence, shakes his head again, and gets up from his chair and leaves your office without another word.

REFLECT ON THIS

* What could you do or have you done in such situations? If you were in the instructor's place as noted in the scenario above, what is the first thing you need to do?
* What resources are available on your campus or elsewhere at your institution or in your community to help Jake?
* Has your college developed a procedure for dealing with urgent issues such as these?
* What role might your campus security force play in such a situation?

As you consider the specific reflection questions above, you may wish to give broader thought to the following:

* What VISION do you have regarding how to recognize and address the nonacademic challenges your students bring to the classroom?
* What specific CHALLENGES exist regarding this topic?
* What ACTION will you take to address the challenges and move toward your vision?
* What RESOURCES will you need?

CONSIDER THIS

Like the previous scenario, the story of Jake reminds us that we do teach so much more than our disciplines. Whether you teach at a community college or a four-year university, your students will bring a variety of issues into your classroom. This is another of those many student situations that underscores the need for a strong bridge between faculty and student services/affairs. If you don't have such collaboration on your campus, find a way to start the conversation. Your students need and deserve it. Students, like Jake, feel vulnerable. You may be the one connection with whom they feel comfortable enough to share their concerns and trepidations.[25] To whom on your campus can you turn in such situations?

You and your faculty colleagues might consider inviting your student services counselors and advisors to discuss this scenario. Perhaps you can also draw in your psychology faculty for input. For me, Jake's story is a reminder that many (most?) faculty members are not trained to handle such crises. Who on your campus serve as the go-to people (departments) for students like Jake? Do those resource people serve as a training resource for faculty?

• • •

Does your college have a strong bridge between faculty and student affairs counselors and advisors?

• • •

Applying The Seven Rs

Before you move on to the next scenario, revisit the seven Rs. What connection(s) can you make between the material presented in this scenario and each of the seven Rs? Once you have completed that, star the principle (the one "R") that seems to be the most significant in this context and reflect on why you believe this is the most significant principle.

* Relationships
* Relevance
* Rainbows

- Resources
- Responsibility
- Reflection
- Resilience

SCENARIO 9

I Don't Have Time for
Games and Complaints

• • •

Organizing Question: What effective strategies can instructors use to connect their students to the excitement of their courses?

Go to www.stevepiscitelli.com for supporting video.

PROFESSOR ADAM HAS TO TEACH one section of a science class for non-science majors this term. Most (if not all) of these students will simply be in the class to satisfy a college general education requirement. The professor has an excellent reputation in the field and at the school for his knowledge of the subject matter. He generally teaches upper-level classes to science majors. In fact, he has not taught a general education class in almost a decade.

"I drew the short straw this semester," he recently told you (a colleague) when discussing his course load for the semester. "What a waste of my time and expertise to be spending time every week with a group of nonscience majors. They have no clue about the elegance and mystery of science. They typically lack any sense of curiosity. They just want to know if this 'will be on the test'! Most of them don't even know why they are in college—let alone understand why they need a science class. They better be ready, I can tell you that," he said as he wagged his finger in your face.

"I have my lectures prepared. All I can say is they better buckle up and be prepared for the demands of science. I don't have time for games and complaints. I fear this will be a long, long semester for me—and them."

REFLECT ON THIS

* What wisdom do you have to pass along to your colleague, Professor Adam?
* Does a class with non-majors require a different approach and strategy than a class for students who major in the subject area?
* What strategies can you suggest to engage the students in such classes as Professor Adam has to teach?
* Is there a way to structure a class for non-majors to help engage students who, according to the professor, have "no clue about the elegance and mystery of science and typically lack any sense of curiosity"?
* What real-life relevant situations or news events can help non-science majors connect to the course material?

As you consider the specific reflection questions above, you may wish to give broader thought to the following:

* What VISION do you have regarding how to connect your students to the "elegance and mysteries" of your discipline?
* What specific CHALLENGES exist regarding this topic?
* What ACTION will you take to address the challenges and move toward your vision?
* What RESOURCES will you need?

CONSIDER THIS

The first thing to consider here is whether or not, generally speaking, we can change a person's attitude. That goes for students and teachers alike. Al Siebert in *The Resiliency Advantage* reminds us that "it takes a long time to develop an attitude, and it takes conscious, applied personal effort to undo or change an attitude." [26] So, probably, just telling your colleague that he needs to change his attitude and think of the positives involved with teaching a general education section might fall on deaf ears. You may want to attempt to appeal to his cognitive, emotional, and behavioral beliefs about this particular situation. Here are a few thoughts:

* Appeal to his stated love for the mystery and elegance of science and ask him how he came to be so excited, curious, and passionate about the subject matter.
* Ask him if he can remember an undergraduate course he took as a student that he *did not* like. What did that professor do to help him—or hinder him in developing a love for the class? Could he do the same for his students?
* What can he do (an experiment, perhaps) that would dramatically show the mystery and elegance of his course?
* Can he share professional learning experiences with his students?

I taught (among other courses) undergraduate US history classes. These courses satisfied general education requirements. The vast majority of my students, when asked the first day about their experience with history classes, would say something to the effect of "I don't do history." When I dug deeper, generally I found they had had poor experiences in prior history classes. Not only did I *tell* them that history had relevance to their lives, I would *show* them that relevance each and every class session. (If I did not, then I did not reach one of my goals for that class session.)

Showing how the course you teach relates to their lives and dreams off campus can, at least, give you a head start in connecting what may seem to students as arcane information with little importance to their reality. And it may help your students develop a cursory curiosity for the material.

• • •

What did your professors do to help you develop enthusiasm and excitement for a class?

• • •

APPLYING THE SEVEN RS

Before you move on to the next scenario, revisit the seven Rs. What connection(s) can you make between the material presented in this scenario and each of the seven Rs? Once you have completed that, star the principle (the one "R") that seems to be the most significant in this context and reflect on why you believe this is the most significant principle.

* Relationships
* Relevance
* Rainbows
* Resources
* Responsibility
* Reflection
* Resilience

I Got an "A" Last Semester!§§

• • •

Organizing Question: If grade inflation exists, what can be done to address it?

Go to www.stevepiscitelli.com for supporting video.

THE FOLLOWING SCENARIO TAKES PLACE on an urban college campus. The school has an open admission policy. And their Vice President for Academics has said, "We accept the top one hundred percent of our applicants." As you read the situation below, consider how you would advise this professor.

"I'm so sick and tired of underprepared students with overinflated values of themselves," railed Professor Kepler. "Just file this under Grade Inflation! It cheapens every discipline, but it's downright deadly in the math and sciences. You know, a student simply cannot do second-semester math without mastering first-semester math. Just that simple. From what I see each semester, I suspect that seventy to eighty percent of students don't have the skills they need."

"As a result," he said to his department chair, "I spend WAY too much time going over stuff that should already have been covered and not enough time getting them ready for the next class after me. I am astounded by how little they know."

"But the real kicker," the professor continued as he paced the office, "is when I am told: 'But I got an A in my last class!'"

---

§§ Thanks to Professor Matt Mitchell of Florida State College at Jacksonville for the inspiration for this scenario.

As he plopped down into a chair, he looked at his department head and complained, "And then I'm the bad guy, the ineffective teacher, when my failure rate is high. What in the world am I supposed to do?"

Reflect on This

* How would you handle this situation if you were the:
  * Professor
  * Department chair
  * Retention specialist
* If grade inflation does exist, what are the reasons for its existence?
* If grade inflation does exist, what can be done to address it?
* Have grades (A–F) become obsolete and meaningless? If they have, with what should they be replaced?
* What influence, if any, should student grades have in faculty evaluations?

As you consider the specific reflection questions above, you may wish to give broader thought to the following:

* What VISION do you have regarding how to address the concerns about grade inflation?
* What specific CHALLENGES exist regarding this topic?
* What ACTION will you take to address the challenges and move toward your vision?
* What RESOURCES will you need?

Consider This

Does grade inflation actually exist? One extensive study pinpoints two eras of high grade inflation: the Vietnam War Era and the Student as Consumer

Era (1980s to present era). The grade of "A," according to this researcher is the most common grade now at both four and two-year institutions.[27]

Some of the reasons you might have heard explaining why grade inflation exists may include:

- Inflated high school grades do not equip the students with the experience of non "A" grades at the collegiate level.
- The student as "customer" mentality sets up the expectation that the "customer" (that is, the student) is always right.
- Higher tuition costs have parents clamoring to get what they paid for (high grades).
- Student evaluations of faculty—and the use of those evaluations for tenure, promotion, or renewal of contract.
- Student are obsessed with the belief that nothing less than an "A" will do for graduate school.
- A larger reliance (at community colleges) on adjunct instructors—and their concern for job retention.
- Concern by full-time faculty about how low grades (Ds and Fs) might affect their job evaluations.
- Lack of consistent standards across departments or disciplines.

If it does exist, where does the inflation exist? Interesting anecdotal observation: When the charge of grade inflation is leveled, it generally appears to be aimed at the *previous* classes or instructors. Do you ever hear your colleagues say openly, "I inflate grades on a regular basis!"? Maybe. The finger, generally, tends to point to another colleague, another campus, or another school.

If it does exist, what have been the consequences of grade inflation, and what do we do about it? The topics of resilience and student success cannot be overlooked. If students do think that "only an 'A'" is equivalent with success, then how does the institution address student "meltdowns" because they "only got a B!"? Do we need to address fragile egos?

If a student got an "A" in a feeder course and is struggling in the next level, is that because of grade inflation or does the current instructor deserve some scrutiny as well? Or does the challenge simply represent the increased difficulty of the course material?

Can grade inflation be attributed to "academic freedom"? That is, since each instructor can establish what she believes is the best way to gauge and rank progress for her students, might there be a large disparity in range of grades and expectations of effort?

Should there be agreed-upon departmental objectives, standards, performance benchmarks, and/or assessments?

What is the connection, if any, between grades issued and faculty evaluations?

• • •

If grade inflation does exist, what are the
consequences of grade inflation?

• • •

APPLYING THE SEVEN RS

Before you move on to the next scenario, revisit the seven Rs. What connection(s) can you make between the material presented in this scenario and each of the seven Rs? Once you have completed that, star the principle (the one "R") that seems to be the most significant in this context and reflect on why you believe this is the most significant principle.

* Relationships
* Relevance
* Rainbows
* Resources
* Responsibility
* Reflection
* Resilience

Grading Fairly and with Effective Feedback

• • •

Organizing Question: How do you strike a balance between candor and caring when it comes to student feedback and evaluation?

Go to www.stevepiscitelli.com for supporting video.

IN HIS WEEKLY REFLECTIVE PRACTICE journal, Professor Capote always focuses on a critical incident in his teaching. Today, he wrote the following in his journal:

> *This past week I returned student essays. Most students did well; a few turned in woefully inadequate work. Most of the sub-par work reflected a lack of basic English skills, skills that should have been learned in high school and/or in previous college coursework. Candor and professional integrity dictate that I must point out the deficiencies. How can they improve if they do not know where they went wrong?*
>
> *And don't I have to balance my candor with care? So, while the students may be shocked, hurt, and disappointed with their poor grades, I do provide opportunities (a second chance) for them to improve their skills. Is that a correct approach—or will the second chance encourage*

sloppy work on their part in the future? They can earn a higher grade on their subsequent effort—but they will have to work with a tutor, consult with a study partner, or visit with me for pointers. Again, I hope they apply what they learn from the opportunity to rewrite their drafts. I don't believe in "giving points" for their "effort." I need to see results! After all, isn't that what college is about—goals and outcomes?

REFLECT ON THIS

* Have you had similar dilemmas arise? If so, how did you handle those situations?
* What do you think about the students' opportunity to "earn a higher grade"?
* What part (if any) of the evaluation process should be based on "effort" put forth by the student?
* Reflect on Professor Capote's reflective practice (weekly journal). What benefits do you see? Any challenges?
* Should the students be required to keep their own weekly journals about their classroom experiences and any questions they have about their progress?

As you consider the specific reflection questions above, you may wish to give broader thought to the following:

* What VISION do you have about providing effective feedback for student growth?
* What specific CHALLENGES exist regarding this topic?
* What ACTION will you take to address the challenges and move toward your vision?
* What RESOURCES will you need?

Consider This

Effective teachers (who are, after all, leaders of the classroom) can balance care and candor. They can establish and maintain validating connections with their students while holding them to a high standard of content mastery and skill development.

Like Professor Capote above, I too provided opportunities for my students to improve their skills. They could earn, on occasion, a higher grade—but they had to work with a tutor, consult with a study partner, or visit with me for assistance and clarification. So, while the students might have been shocked, hurt, and disappointed with their poor grades, I did my best to create teachable moments.

My goal was not simply to raise their grades (that would be misdirected compassion and potential grade inflation. See Scenario 10). I wanted to raise their skill and grit levels. If they addressed their weaknesses (pointed out with honesty), improved grades could follow.

When students are passed along with minimal competency—because of so-called caring for the student or concern for the institution's retention rates—no one gains. We cheapen our course, we denigrate the degree/certificate, the students' work ethic suffers, and we have to question the impact on the (future) community workforce.[28]

There have been reports about faculty feeling pressured to give higher grades than students deserve.[29] Is this a conversation that needs to be approached within your institutional culture?

It is one thing to say our students should raise themselves up with hard work. We need to help them with specific feedback on their strengths, challenges, and resource availability.

Caring without candor. Candor without caring. Either one can raise significant concerns.[30]

• • •

There always existed a teachable moment.

• • •

Applying The Seven Rs

Before you move on to the next scenario, revisit the seven Rs. What connection(s) can you make between the material presented in this scenario and each of the seven Rs? Once you have completed that, star the principle (the one "R") that seems to be the most significant in this context and reflect on why you believe this is the most significant principle.

* Relationships
* Relevance
* Rainbows
* Resources
* Responsibility
* Reflection
* Resilience

The Case for Mentoring First-Year Faculty

• • •

Organizing Question: What needs to be emphasized and who needs to be involved for a faculty mentoring program to be considered effective?

Go to www.stevepiscitelli.com for supporting video.

SHILA IS A FACULTY MEMBER at a large (more than forty thousand students) state college in the southeastern region of the United States. In her most previous position (at the same college), Shila served as a program manager for the ESOL program for four years. While she enjoyed her management role, she yearned to be in the classroom. (She had previous full-time and adjunct teaching credentials.) When a full-time/tenured professorship became available, she applied and was hired. Even though it meant a reduction in pay, she was "over the moon" about her career decision. She started her new full-time faculty position in the spring semester.

The good news for Shila was that she knew the ins and outs (procedurally) of the campus and the college. She knew the college culture and politics. And the campus knew her (positively). So far, so good. However, even though Shila had had previous teaching experience, she was embarking on a new adventure. Her load consisted of five classes—some that she had taught in the past and some with which she had minimal experience.

She had trepidation about the load—and, frankly, how she would fit in now as a peer in a department she once managed.

This college does *not* have a uniformed faculty mentoring program. Shila's dean asked a veteran teacher if he would be interested in mentoring Shila —and he asked Shila if she would like to participate in a mentoring relationship. Both enthusiastically agreed. Other than intrinsic rewards, there would be no other remuneration.

The mentor, Steve, is a master teacher on campus. He is completing his thirty-third year of teaching in the social and behavioral sciences. At the completion of this spring semester, Steve will retire from the college. He, also, has been serving as a faculty development coordinator on the campus, and he teaches four classes (history and student success).

Without any formal faculty mentoring training, Steve met with Shila to discuss what Shila wanted from the relationship. He suggested a few paths they could travel—but left the direction to what Shila needed/wanted to discuss. They set up a regular one-hour weekly meeting (Mondays from 2:30 to 3:30 p.m. in the campus café). Additionally, since their offices were next to each other, they dropped in on each other for informal chats. Other than keeping the dean informed that they were meeting, their conversations remained confidential.

Over the course of the sixteen-week semester, Shila and Steve treated their meeting time as sacrosanct. Even when they missed the regular meetings (one time Steve was at a conference; one time Shila was ill; one time there was a department meeting), they rescheduled. Additionally, Shila volunteered to participate in a three-hour reflective practice workshop Steve facilitated for campus faculty. They found their meetings professionally rewarding.

Their conversations never lagged, and each session went for the full sixty minutes. Topics ranged from collegial interactions, critical classroom incidents, department dynamics, the importance of basic principles of student success, personal resilience, priority management, and personal wealth-building strategies. Steve observed part of one of

Shila's classes and provided her with a detailed written report of that visit.

There was no formal preassessment or survey of this mentoring relationship. There was a formal exit feedback questionnaire that Shila completed at the end of the semester. Additionally, they regularly spoke of the bright spots and not-so bright spots of their mentoring relationships. Shila believed, for instance, that this mentoring relationship gave her an ongoing opportunity to share (and sometimes vent) and get feedback on her teaching journey. While the entirety of the experience was highly beneficial, Shila thought about losing Steve as a resource once he retired from the college at the end of the semester. She had thought out loud that maybe a second semester of mentoring (with less frequent meetings) might have been beneficial.

REFLECT ON THIS
Practical Planning for the Future: A Top Ten

* Does the campus (college) need a recognized and ongoing mentoring program?
* While this mentor-mentee pairing worked extremely well, what should be the rubric for future pairings? Should there be a rubric?
* To what extent should the confidentiality of the mentor-mentee relationship be maintained in future mentoring relationships?
* How should the mentoring relationship be monitored—and by whom? Should it be monitored?
* How long should the "formal" relationship last—one semester? Less? More?
* Should there be a formalized preassessment and postassessment of the mentoring relationship?
* Should there be incentives (money, recognition, other) for participation in the program for the mentor?

- Should this be a mandated program for the mentee?
- What percentage of the mentoring emphasis should be functional/ procedural, cultural/political, pedagogical or other?
- What happens if the mentor and mentee find out they don't like working in the relationship?[31]

As you consider the specific reflection questions above, you may wish to give broader thought to the following:

- What VISION do you have for effective faculty mentoring?
- What specific CHALLENGES exist regarding this topic?
- What ACTION will you take to address the challenges and move toward your vision?
- What RESOURCES will you need?

Consider This

Onboarding/orienting/mentoring new faculty into the teaching ranks remains one of the more important tasks in education. Think about the hundreds of hours that go into *selecting* a faculty member to fill a teaching position. Add up the hours (for all the people involved in the process) the application screening, the generation of interview questions, the phone calls, the final interviews, and the campus visits. Then consider how much time is invested in acclimating the new hire to the teaching and learning culture of the institution. Are there any disconnections?

At your institution is there an actual mentoring program in place for faculty? I see mentoring as a piece of the onboarding process. Giving a new hire the keys, a copy of the procedure manual, and a copy of the campus safety plan, while important, is not mentoring per se. Mentoring connotes an ongoing relationship between a novice to the campus (or the calling) and someone with wisdom and ability to build a nurturing and mutually respectful relationship.

The ten items above ("Reflect on This" section) provide a broad look at a some concerns for a faculty mentoring program to consider.

Again, as with all programming, consider how your mentoring program will develop. Will a mentoring program (with its associated objectives and time lines) be developed "on high" and dictated to the faculty? Will faculty have meaningful input into mentoring competencies? In other words, will your institution develop a mentoring program and then "sell" it to the faculty? Or will the faculty have input into the development of the program before it's developed?

Has your institution surveyed both veteran and "rookie" faculty to see what they found beneficial and/or lacking in their onboarding process to the institution and campus?

Once you have commitment to a faculty mentoring program and someone who will lead the effort, perhaps the most practical next step is to develop your mentoring program's purpose. Why does your college or university need it, and what do you want it to accomplish? How do you know the purpose is appropriate?

Whether your institution has a long-standing program or is in the process of developing one, look around your state and the nation for ideas of what has worked and has not worked. Examine what you can adapt, tweak, or create. Survey current faculty. Ask them what kind of guidance they wished they had had in their first year on campus.

Whatever form your faculty mentoring program takes, remember that your program helps to create the future for your college and your students.[32]

• • •

Onboarding new faculty into the teaching ranks remains one of the more important tasks in education.

• • •

APPLYING THE SEVEN RS

Before you move on to the next scenario, revisit the seven Rs. What connection(s) can you make between the material presented in this scenario and each of the seven Rs? Once you have completed that, star the principle (the one "R") that seems to be the most significant in this context and reflect on why you believe this is the most significant principle.

* Relationships
* Relevance
* Rainbows
* Resources
* Responsibility
* Reflection
* Resilience

Encouraging and Challenging All Students with Instructional Strategies

• • •

Organizing Question: What can an instructor do to encourage all students to respond in a meaningful and relevant manner during a class session?

Go to www.stevepiscitelli.com for supporting video.

IT'S THE SECOND WEEK OF the semester. All of Professor Hopper's students are in place. This includes three students who missed the first week due to various reasons. (One student had financial-aid issues, a second registered late, and the third had childcare challenges.)

So, at this point, all students have the syllabus, and the class is underway. Students are in place, and the professor is headlong into her content.

As she reviews her class attendance sheet prior to class one day, she notes that there are basically three types of students in her class:

1. Johnny represents the first type. He enters the class right as the professor is about to begin. He has not offered any responses in class. He looks exhausted each day as he drifts in and out of slumber in the back row.

2. Andrea was the first one into class on day one. Very animatedly she made her way to the front row. There she pulled out

her new tablet *and* laptop. She announced that she was ready to learn and get her degree. She excitedly talked about all five of her classes. By the end of week two, you can already see a change. She seems a bit overwhelmed; she has lost her initial excitement. Today she raised her hand and asked if she could turn her assignment in late.

3. Tyrone has not lost any of the excitement or energy he started with just two weeks ago. He comes to class five minutes early each day. Professor Hopper notices that Tyrone always engages in appropriate conversation with his classmates and has offered to start a study group for the weekly quizzes. He has already visited the professor's office to say, "Hi."

Professor Hopper has noticed something about her teaching as well. After asking Johnny a few questions—and receiving little more than a grunt in response—she finds herself directing her questions to Tyrone and his group of study friends. They always respond and bring so much energy to the class. "They validate my efforts," she told a colleague after a recent class. She has so much content to cover that she finds that she really doesn't have time to get bogged down drawing answers from students who are distracted or lack interest.

"If Johnny wants to sleep, there isn't much I can do," the professor offered. "It's his tuition and his time. Maybe he is just unsure of himself and will come around after watching the good behaviors of Tyrone and his friends. And then there's Andrea. I see her type of student in every class. They come in all excited with great intentions and a full class schedule. But they have absolutely no stamina. She bit off more than she can handle with five classes. I think it would be best for her to see an advisor and withdraw from two or three classes.

"Thank God for Tyrone. He is keeping the class afloat. I'm thinking of giving him a few extra credit points for all of his efforts. He is wonderful!

"Am I wrong? Am I missing something here?" She came to you for feedback.

Reflect on This

* Consider how and what Professor Hopper did in her class. If you had to give her collegial feedback, what would you say about the following?
    * Johnny. Would you just ignore him? After all, he is an adult and can make his own decisions. Why might he be acting in this manner? What would you say to Johnny? Or would you ignore him and let him sleep? Why do you think he behaves in the way he does? Are campus resources available that might help Johnny?
    * Andrea. Why is she losing energy and focus already? Is it simply because she has too many classes? Is dropping a class or two the only option? Does she need priority management training? Are there other issues?
    * Tyrone. What do you think about Professor Hopper's comments that Tyrone "validates" her and she is thinking of giving him extra credit? Can he become a model student for the class?
    * Anything else Professor Hopper could have done better—or needs to do now?
    * Anything she did particularly well?

As you consider the specific reflection questions above, you may wish to give broader thought to the following:

* What VISION do you have for engaging students of varying abilities, interests, and attitudes?
* What specific CHALLENGES exist regarding this topic?
* What ACTION will you take to address the challenges and move toward your vision?
* What RESOURCES will you need?

Consider This

As cliché as it sounds, you will have all types of students in your classes. Consider the following demonstration I did for my students on the first day of the semester.

I place a glass of water into the hands of three students (each student has her own glass of water).[33] Into the first glass I drop an aspirin; glass two gets the type of effervescent tablet that explodes with bubbles and fizz; and into the third I drop a tablet that is used to clean dentures (it fizzes and changes the color of the water). Each tablet represents the types of students (and issues) that can walk through our classroom doors.

- Student 1 (represented by the aspirin): Sits there. Not much happening—not much in the way of participation or other form of engagement. Not much impact on the environment. No splash of any kind. Not much energy. Nothing seems to change.

- Student 2 (represented by the effervescent tablet): Makes an initial splash. Energetic, participatory, and probably has all the technological tools (smartphone, tablet, and laptop). He may even sit in the first couple rows of the classroom. The initial enthusiasm gives way around weeks three or four. Feeling overwhelmed with all he has bitten off this semester, he starts getting to class late and missing assignments. He cannot sustain the initial momentum.

- Student 3 (represented by the denture-cleaning tablet): Starts off strong and eventually begins to make changes that are visible (more confident; consistently high assignment and test grades; leadership role in class, for example). Not only does he or she grow with his or her changes, he or she has an impact on the class as well.

And keep in mind that it is possible for all three tablets to be a metaphor for the student who starts off reticent and reserved, then gets a spurt of energy and inspiration, and eventually is a change agent for himself and the classroom (and maybe even the campus).

A teacher's calling is to recognize each of these types (and more) and reach out with encouragement and challenge.[34] It will require differentiated approaches. And it will require effort.

As for Professor Hopper (in this scenario), here are a few thoughts to consider:

- Johnny. Letting him drift off to sleep is not the best choice here. Yes, he makes his choices, but there are a few things to consider. For one, is he sleeping because of late-night partying and limited sleep—or is there a health or substance abuse problem? Does she know for sure he is not a risk to himself or others in the classroom? Or is it possible Johnny's sleepiness might be due to an all-night job he needs to support his family? Why is he in this particular class? Does he feel intimidated and anxious? Or has he enrolled in the wrong class for him at this time in his college career? Does it matter why he drifts off to sleep?

- Andrea. Besides the five classes, what else is going on in her life? Are there childcare or financial issues—that maybe the college could help with? Perhaps she just needs a little help identifying and organizing her priorities. Does she have a history of weak grit and perseverance? Has she enrolled in a class inappropriate for her skill level? Should Professor Hopper offer to help her?

- Tyrone. Since Tyrone is motivated (and appears to know the material) and passionate, is there any harm in letting him be the leader in class participation? Can he be a role model—or could he possibly stifle discussion? Will other students just let him answer? What can the professor do to encourage other students to participate in class?

This would be an appropriate scenario to use with your new faculty training/mentoring or as a kick-off scenario for the beginning of the new academic year for all faculty.

• • •

***A teacher's calling is to reach out with
encouragement and challenge.***

• • •

Applying The Seven Rs

Before you move on to the next scenario, revisit the seven Rs. What connection(s) can you make between the material presented in this scenario and each of the seven Rs? Once you have completed that, star the principle (the one "R") that seems to be the most significant in this context and reflect on why you believe this is the most significant principle.

* Relationships
* Relevance
* Rainbows
* Resources
* Responsibility
* Reflection
* Resilience

Boundaries and Limits

• • •

Organizing Question: Have you established clear boundaries and limits with your colleagues and students?

Go to www.stevepiscitelli.com for supporting video.

PROFESSOR ROGER BELL RETURNED TO his campus office after completing his first day of his first semester as a first-year classroom teacher. He placed his books and class folder on his desk, pulled a bottle of water from his lunch bag, and sat down at his computer. As he took a sip of water, he scrolled through the emails that had poured into his inbox since earlier that morning. A knock on the door interrupted his thoughts. He looked up and saw his department chair, Dr. Tony Marconi, smiling at him.

"Well, how did things go for you today, Rog? I know you were well prepared for your three full sections of students." Marconi pulled up a chair in front of Roger's desk.

"Actually, I felt pretty good. I was a bit nervous to start, but, you know, the new faculty training that I attended at the teaching and learning center really paid off. They gave me a lot of practical strategies that helped me today. There were, however, a few things that caught me off guard."

He offered a bottle of water, and Dr. Marconi accepted. "What kind of things?" the department chair asked and then unscrewed the cap and drank some water.

"Well, a few students seemed to be surprised that I did not provide them with my cell-phone number. They said that email was 'yesterday's way to communicate.' They wanted me to provide my number so we could have timely conversations or text-message exchanges if they had questions or might miss class. I don't feel comfortable doing that. I need separation between class and private life. When I explained that, they just stared at me. And I interpreted 'timely' to mean they wanted 'immediate' responses to what they perceived as their special requests." Roger leaned across his desk and continued.

"One of my students approached me after class and said that she had looked me up on Facebook after she had registered for the class. She wanted to know if I got her 'friend' request. Again, I'm not comfortable with this. But I don't want to hurt her feelings. She seems like a genuinely friendly young woman."

"And," Roger said as he waved his hand at the computer screen, "I see I just got a request from the student activities director. He wants to know if I would be willing to sponsor the forensics club. You know that I've already agreed to sit on two committees. I don't want to come across as a complainer, but I have to have some time for me to just be me."

Roger sat back, looked at his department chair, and asked, "What would you do if you were me with these requests?"

REFLECT ON THIS

* What compelling reasons, if any, exist for Professor Bell to provide his personal phone number to students?
* What compelling reasons, if any, exist for Professor Bell *not* to give his personal phone number to students?
* What about social-media "friend" requests from students? Is this appropriate or professional? Does your institution have a policy about social media in general and teacher-student relationships on social media in particular?

- What would you do, if you were Professor Bell, and you got the request from the student activities director to sponsor a club?
- Does the fact that the professor is a first-year instructor have any bearing on your responses?

As you consider the specific reflection questions above, you may wish to give broader thought to the following:

- What VISION do you have concerning appropriate boundaries and limits for your students and colleagues?
- What specific CHALLENGES exist regarding this topic?
- What ACTION will you take to address the challenges and move toward your vision?
- What RESOURCES will you need?

CONSIDER THIS

In his book *The Anger Solution: The Proven Method for Achieving Calm and Developing Healthy, Long-Lasting Relationships*, author John Lee distinguishes between *boundaries* and *limits*.[35]

Boundaries show where we "begin and end," according to Lee. They let others know what is acceptable and unacceptable. They tell people how far they can go with another person. When boundaries are clearly established, there is no ambiguity.

Example: Dominic takes Marie on a date. Nice dinner, movie, a couple of drinks later in the evening. Marie let Dominick know *before* the date that this would be an evening to enjoy each other's company—but nothing else. No invitation to come inside; no sexual encounter. Just dinner and conversation and friendship. That is a clearly set boundary. Marie has let Dominic know what acceptable and unacceptable behavior is on the date.

Example: Professor Serra tells his students they can contact him by email or his campus phone. He will answer students as soon as he possibly can. He, however, will not take any phone calls at his home or on his personal cell phone. He has set a clear boundary for his students.

Example: The dean expects all faculty to be present for the department meeting. That is, they need to be physically *and* mentally in the room. The new rule (the boundary): All phones will be in the OFF position. There will be NO texting, NO phone calls, and NO web surfing during a meeting. NO exceptions!

According to Lee, boundaries help tell people where *they* can go or not go as it relates to you. They provide clear demarcations and avoid guessing games. Or at least, they should.

Limits let people know how far *you* will go. They clearly tell people what you will do or will not do. If established correctly, people are not left guessing about what to expect from you. People without clearly established limits can end up giving more (physically, emotionally, occupationally) than they want to give. This can result in resentment, hurt feelings, or even rage. But you do it to yourself.

Example: Joan has a son, Johnny, who is in middle school. She gladly and lovingly makes him a nutritious lunch each day. However, lately, Josh forgets his lunch two or three times a week. He calls home from school, and Joan runs the lunch to him. Finally, Joan told Johnny she would no longer bring his lunch to school. If he forgets it, he will not have lunch that day. Sure enough, the next day, Johnny forgot his lunch; he called home, and Joan calmly told him she would not be able to bring his lunch to the school. She had set a limit on what she would do—and she adhered to her limit.

Example. Professor Yotch told her students she will read any and all rough drafts of their papers up to three days before the due date. After that time (her limit) she will not take them, as she will need to devote time to her other class assignments. Anything that comes in after that deadline will be returned to the student without comment. She has maintained this policy for the last four semesters. Her policy is stated in her syllabus.

Example: Jerry has been carpooling with John for the past few months. John insists on talking on his cell phone and texting while driving. Jerry has told John this is not safe (the limit) and has asked him to stop. John continues his unsafe practices. Jerry will no longer carpool with John.

Boundaries are for others, and limits are for you. As I read Lee's book, I thought about the times that I had been angry and frustrated with others because they caused me to lose time, work late, or take on extra tasks. In many of those instances, as I think back, it was because I did not establish a clear boundary for them or a clear limit for myself. Boundaries and limits can be adjusted along the way based on additional information. But for them to be effective and healthy, they have to be clear to both us and those with whom we live and work.

• • •

Boundaries are for others and limits are for you.

• • •

Applying The Seven Rs

Before you move on to the next scenario, revisit to the seven Rs. What connection(s) can you make between the material presented in this scenario and each of the seven Rs? Once you have completed that, star the principle (the one "R") that seems to be the most significant in this context and reflect on why you believe this is the most significant principle.

* Relationships
* Relevance
* Rainbows
* Resources
* Responsibility
* Reflection
* Resilience

Student Attendance

• • •

Organizing Question: Should instructors have an attendance policy, and should it be strictly adhered to each class meeting for the entire semester?

Go to www.stevepiscitelli.com for supporting video.

PROFESSOR MCGEE HAS JUST COMPLETED the first meeting of her Anatomy and Physiology class. It meets twice a week, seventy-five minutes each meeting, for a sixteen-week semester. "Not a bad beginning," she thought as she packed up her books before heading back toward her office. "They were engaged, civil, and, for the most part, on-task. Only a few latecomers."

As she signed off the classroom computer, Alex approached her and asked if he could speak with her for a few minutes.

"Sure, how can I help you? Remind me of your name, please?"

"It's Alex. First, I want to tell you how excited I am to be in your class this semester. You have a great reputation with the students. Second, I apologize for being late. Please do not take that as disrespect."

"I understand. Sometimes the first day of class can be a bit overwhelming what with finding a parking spot and locating the classroom. Starting next class period, though, I have zero tolerance for tardiness. The class starts at 9:30 a.m.—not 9:31 a.m. We have a great deal to cover in class, and students need to be here for the entire class period." Professor McGee said this firmly and with a smile. She wanted to make her point while not sounding rude. She believed punctuality was a nonnegotiable point for her class.

"Well," said a somewhat chagrined Alex, "that's what I was hoping to talk with you about. You see, I have this job. I'm a single dad of one very cute six-year-old girl, Laurie. The job is our only source of income. The problem is your class ends at 10:45 a.m. I have to be at work promptly at 11:00 a.m. Now the good news is that it's just a few miles away. So I know I can get there in plenty of time if I leave class at 10:30 each day. I'll sit in the back of the room so as not to disturb anyone. And my buddy, Nicky, is also in the class. He has already agreed to take notes for me. So, this will be OK, right?"

REFLECT ON THIS

- List the various options Professor McGee has in this situation.
- For each option you list above, do the following:
  - What assumptions connect to the options—by the professor and the student?
  - What are the positive consequences/implications of each option?
  - What are the negative consequences/implications of each option?
- Which option would you follow—and why do you think that is the most appropriate option?
- What other circumstances (other than work-related issues) might students present regarding attendance? How might you respond to those?

As you consider the specific reflection questions above, you may wish to give broader thought to the following:

- What VISION do you have regarding student attendance?
- What specific CHALLENGES exist regarding this topic?

- What ACTION will you take to address the challenges and move toward your vision?
- What RESOURCES will you need?

CONSIDER THIS

A host of questions present themselves that Professor McGee may want to consider:

- Is there a department or college-wide policy on attendance? If not, should there be?
- Is there a requirement in place (by the college or the program of study) that stipulates how many hours the student must attend the class in order to be eligible for credit?
- Is "getting the notes" the main point here?
- Should the fact that Alex is a single parent even come into consideration when it comes to class expectations and rigor?
- Are punctuality and attendance "nonnegotiables" for a college class?
- Does the type of class or discipline make a difference as to whether or not this student request should be granted?
- Is regular attendance and punctuality just "so yesterday"? Is required classroom attendance an antiquated habit that was important in the industrial society but not in our postindustrial society with virtual online educational opportunities?
- Is there a connection between classroom attendance and punctuality and the workplace?

Many semesters I had to address the exact request Alex raises in this scenario. I (like Professor McGee) saw punctuality and class attendance as a nonnegotiable trait that would be important in the world of work. One way to approach this type of situation is to turn the scenario around for the student. Often, I would propose the following to the student:

Alex, I appreciate you coming to me with this situation on the first day. I have a suggestion. Tell your boss that you will be able to work Monday, Tuesday, Thursday, and Friday but <u>not</u> Wednesday. And make sure you tell him that even though you cannot work on Wednesdays, you still expect a 100 percent paycheck for the week.

My guess, Alex, is that your boss will not go for that—and you know that. But your request asks me to excuse you from 20 percent of the semester for 100 percent of the semester's credit. The good news is that this is the first day of the semester, and we can see what we can do to get you into another section that will work with your employment.

I never had a student take me up on that. They always found a way to be in class every day for the full time—and tend to their out-of-class responsibilities. It also provided a teaching moment to help the student understand the importance of reaching out to professors *before* enrolling in a class section to address such issues.

One way to treat attendance and punctuality is to view them as workplace habits that reflect respect, seriousness, responsibility, and dedication.

• • •

**She believed punctuality was a nonnegotiable point
for her class.**

• • •

APPLYING THE SEVEN RS

Before you move on to the next scenario, revisit the seven Rs. What connection(s) can you make between the material presented in this scenario and each of the seven Rs? Once you have completed that, star the principle (the one "R") that seems to be the most significant in this context and reflect on why you believe this is the most significant principle.

- Relationships
- Relevance
- Rainbows
- Resources
- Responsibility
- Reflection
- Resilience

Student Phones, Tablets, and Laptops in Class

• • •

Organizing Question: Should schools be an "open carry" zone when it comes to technology in the classroom?

Go to www.stevepiscitelli.com for supporting video.

"LAST SEMESTER KILLED ME," LAMENTED Professor Amani to his department chair. "I'm all for using technology, and I'm no troglodyte, but enough is enough. The amount of texting and checking social-media sites during class time has gotten out of hand. I even had students answer incoming calls and start talking as they slowly sauntered out of the room—while I was conducting class!"

"Times have changed since we were in school. I've just decided to go with the flow. If I don't see the use and it doesn't bother me, I don't bother with it," said the not-too-excited department chair.

"Well, it does bother me, and that is why I am including this in my syllabus for next semester." The professor slid his draft syllabus, opened to the section titled "Cell Phones and Digital Policy," across the desk to his chair. It read as such:

Our time together in class is valuable. As the professor, I promise you that each day I am in the classroom, my focus will be on the class. I will not answer my cell phone. I will not make a call from my cell phone. I will not send or read text messages during the class. My attention will be on the class.

I ask the same courtesy of you. Our class does not need disruptions caused by ringing/vibrating cell phones.

Before entering class, silence all cell phones, tablets, and other such devices. Campus security can be reached by family members for emergency phone calls. Please note the following:

* *If you have your cell phone in view during class, if the cell phone rings during class, if you use your phone or send/read a text message during class, and/or if you leave the room to use your phone, the instructor reserves the right to ask you to leave class that day. You will be responsible for getting notes or any other class material missed.*
* *The second time any of the above disruptions occur, your name will be submitted to the dean for appropriate action.*

Laptops may be used for class purposes (notes, Internet search for class discussion). Please do not check your email, social-media sites or use the laptop for any other personal purpose during class. You are on your honor for this.

There will be times when you WILL be allowed to use cell phones and other digital devices to access the Internet during class time. You will be told when the time is appropriate for their use in class. Thank you for your consideration and cooperation.

"It is my classroom. I should be able to put in the syllabi whatever I feel is appropriate in order for the students to learn the subject matter. Will you back me up on this if I am challenged?" asked Professor Amani.

The chair scrunched his lips and thought. "What if a student has a sick child or a relative in the hospital? You know they have the right to carry their cell phones and tablets to class."

"If the situation is that serious, then I suggest the student miss class that day. He or she does not have the right to interrupt me or distract other students. This tethering to the technology has become the latest societal addiction in my opinion![36] Will I be supported if I put this policy into effect?"

REFLECT ON THIS

- You're the department chair. What would you do in this situation?
- Do students have the "right" to receive phone calls and texts in "emergency situations" during the class?
- Is there middle ground here? If so, what is it? If not, why not?
- Is the professor correct in saying that this tethering to technology is "the latest societal addiction"?
- If using technology (for example, a cell phone) was the difference between the student remaining in class (or even school), would that make a difference in your decision?
- Should this be part of the college's retention discussion? Orientation discussion? Instruction discussion?
- Is there a department or campus policy? If not, should there be?
- Can you make connections between the topic in this scenario and the workplace?

As you consider the specific reflection questions above, you may wish to give broader thought to the following:

- What VISION do you have regarding the use of student technology in the college classroom?
- What specific CHALLENGES exist regarding this topic?
- What ACTION will you take to address the challenges and move toward your vision?
- What RESOURCES will you need?

CONSIDER THIS

Digital distractions have become a thorny classroom situation. Nonacademic issues continually have an impact on your students. We live in a highly interconnected world. What role, if any, should the college classroom play in having a discussion about the proper use of technology?

* Should schools be "open carry zones" when it comes to cell phones in the classroom?
* What modeling are faculty providing for their students? That is, are they "addicted" to their phones in the classroom?
* Maybe a discussion about distraction and safety issues would be in order. For instance, a discussion about paying attention to one's surroundings (such as walking to class from the parking lot) may be appropriate.
* What does this kind of tethered-fear-of-missing-out habit say for employability? How about relationships?

I included wording in my syllabi similar to what you find in this scenario. I ran it by both my dean and the Dean of Student Services to make sure I had their support. When I presented it to the students, I did my best not to do it in a finger-wagging and scolding manner. I explained it from two perspectives. (1) This time in class belonged to them. Why allow someone else's agenda (an incoming text or social-media post) interrupt their lives? And (2) they did not have the right to interfere and interrupt the education of their classmates. I had minimal problems with this. The students (for the most part) "got it."

• • •

I should be able to put in the syllabi whatever I feel is appropriate in order for the students to learn.

• • •

Applying The Seven Rs

Before you move on to the next scenario, revisit the seven Rs. What connection(s) can you make between the material presented in this scenario and each of the seven Rs? Once you have completed that, star the principle (the one "R") that seems to be the most significant in this context and reflect on why you believe this is the most significant principle.

* Relationships
* Relevance
* Rainbows
* Resources
* Responsibility
* Reflection
* Resilience

Textbooks

• • •

Organizing Question: Should students be required to buy or rent textbooks?

Go to www.stevepiscitelli.com for supporting video.

PROFESSOR MURRAY'S STUDENTS HAVE JUST completed the second week of the semester, and it is increasingly obvious to her that the students have not been reading their textbook assignments. In fact, she has serious doubts if many students even bought or rented the textbook. Her class is textbook-driven. From in-class group work to out-of-class homework, the students need the textbook. Without it they will have a difficult—if not impossible—time passing the course. She has admonished them each day when they come unprepared. All she seems to get is a plaintive plea like, "Do we really need this overpriced textbook? I'm on a very tight budget!"

Professor Murray has told the students, "Either you get the book or you fail. It's that simple, and the choice is entirely in your hands. Buy it (the textbook) or fail it (the course)!"

Her department chair has suggested that Professor Murray consider moving away from a textbook-driven class.

You are Professor Murray's colleague. She has come to you with the information above and has asked for your thoughts.

Reflect on This

* Do you need more information before you can help your colleague? If so, specifically tell her what else you need to know about this situation?
* Do you agree with Professor Murray's stance ("Buy it or fail it!")? Why or why not?
* What about her department chair's suggestion? How could this be carried out?
* What else would you suggest Professor Murray consider?

As you consider the specific reflection questions above, you may wish to give broader thought to the following:

* What VISION do you have regarding teaching, learning, and the use of textbooks?
* What specific CHALLENGES exist regarding this topic?
* What ACTION will you take to address the challenges and move toward your vision?
* What RESOURCES will you need?

Consider This

When it comes to textbook selection and required readings for students, faculty have options. Consider the following:

* According to The College Board, class textbooks and materials costs average in the neighborhood of $1200 per year for an undergraduate student attending a four-year public college or university.[37] You probably have experienced that some students will not even buy a textbook. Some students claim that textbook cost also can factor into which courses to take and which courses to avoid.

- In 2015, NBC News reported that college textbook prices had risen more than 1,000 percent since 1977.[38] The publishing industry claims the statistic is "misleading."
- Open Source publishing has been touted by professors and colleges as a way to ease the sticker shock for students. Should states mandate the use of open educational resources over traditional required texts and campus bookstore offerings?
- Major publishers will offer options to custom-publish a book. Depending on the arrangement, schools can either mix and match chapters from various authors and/or create their own content. Depending on what the school chooses, this could lower costs for students.
- Faculty can place required readings on "reserve" in the campus library. If this is a viable choice for you and your students, check with your reference librarian. In addition to receiving the material in a timely fashion, make sure there are no publisher prohibitions about placing sources in the library for free checkout and use.[***]

Whatever path you and your colleagues choose to travel, perform due diligence. Price is an important consideration as are other factors. For instance, major publishers can provide supplemental materials such as websites, learning management systems, pre- and postassessments, videos, digital slides, and instructor's manuals. Are any of these important to you and your students? If they are, what would it cost you (your school and the students) to find (or develop) and use such supplements? If your school decides to develop these resources, who will select and vet the internal authors?

Pay attention to the author's credentials, the readability of the text, and the quality of the production. Also, does the book provide access to

---

[***] For a number of semesters, I used to place a copy of the course textbook in the campus library for students who either had financial challenges or for whatever reason could not purchase their own copy in a timely fashion. I had to discontinue that service when our campus reference librarian informed me that publishers had balked at this practice. Check with your library and/or publisher representative for alternatives.

disabled populations? What other considerations are important for your students and for you to deliver the course content? In short, know what you get and what you give up.

You may want to consider whether or not you can have access to the book's author. Will he or she be able to come to campus to speak with you, your colleagues, and students? Is this important to you, your campus, and your students? Will there be a cost for such a connection and visit? As with most anything we use, opportunity costs must be considered.

• • •

*Whatever path you and your colleagues choose
to travel, perform due diligence.*

• • •

Applying The Seven Rs

Before you move on to the next scenario, revisit the seven Rs. What connection(s) can you make between the material presented in this scenario and each of the seven Rs? Once you have completed that, star the principle (the one "R") that seems to be the most significant in this context and reflect on why you believe this is the most significant principle.

* Relationships
* Relevance
* Rainbows
* Resources
* Responsibility
* Reflection
* Resilience

Committee Work

• • •

Organizing Question: In what ways can committee assignments and committee workload be equitably and effectively distributed?

Go to www.stevepiscitelli.com for supporting video.

PROFESSOR DAVIS HAS BEEN THE English department chair for three years. Prior to his appointment, he had been an award-winning faculty member on his campus (and in the same department) for twenty years. He knows the ins and outs of the college culture. He is well-versed in the four Ps of his college: procedures, policies, politics, and pedagogies. And most importantly he is not pedantic. He has a keen observational ability and an effective way to build meaningful relationships with his colleagues.

A second-year faculty member, Associate Professor Andy O'Brian, has come to him with a concern about a college-wide committee he has been appointed to by the dean. "I need a little guidance," O'Brian said as he stepped into Professor Davis's office. "The faculty development committee I am serving on has become a lot of work and emotionally draining."

"Have a seat, Andy. Let's talk." Davis motioned to a side chair for his colleague to sit.

"Well, first the good news," offered the young colleague. "I like most of the people on this committee. Since it is comprised of faculty from all over the college, I have met and gotten to know more of my colleagues.

I am learning about opportunities for professional growth that I did not know about. And people are beginning to know who I am. And I appreciate your confidence to recommend my appointment. All good...to a point."

"And...? What's not so good?" asked his department leader.

"Well, there are ten people on the committee. I am the only newbie, so-to-speak. At the first meeting, Professor Dunnenuff moved that I be named the chair of the committee. It was seconded and unanimously approved. I was stunned but felt I could not say no. Especially since the campus president was present."

Professor Davis nodded. "Yeah, that's pretty standard for her. She likes to give the committee its charge and let the members know she will support them in whatever way possible. She is very authentic about that."

"I know. I did feel validated. But now, I'm exhausted. I'm teaching five classes, as you know. And three are different preparations. I have come to find that I'm doing most of the work on this committee. Other than the first meeting, we barely have had a quorum at succeeding meetings. I am creating the agenda, posting minutes, and doing most of the work. Everyone else just kind of sits there. They are pleasant but nonparticipatory. When I have gently said something about this, I was told that this was excellent training for me. They all laugh good-naturedly and say it will look good in my tenure portfolio. I am at the point where I am starting to resent this—and I feel I have no recourse. I'm stuck and not liking it."

REFLECT ON THIS

* As a relatively new faculty member, how would you address a similar issue with your committee or department chair?
* If you are the department chair, how do you advise Associate Professor O'Brian?
* Should the professor speak up to his committee members more forcefully? What would you suggest he say to the committee?

* Should he just do the work and be done with it? Kind of accept it as a rite of passage?
* Is this fair? Does "fair" even matter?

As you consider the specific reflection questions above, you may wish to give broader thought to the following:

* What VISION do you have regarding committee assignments and participation on your campus?
* What specific CHALLENGES exist regarding this topic?
* What ACTION will you take to address the challenges and move toward your vision?
* What RESOURCES will you need?

Consider This

During my college tenure, full-time faculty at my institution had an expectation to devote a specific number of hours per week to committee and college service. This was a contractual obligation. Perhaps your institution has the same responsibilities spelled out for faculty.

When (not if) you find yourself engaged in committee work, understand your role on the committee. In the scenario above, Associate Professor O'Brian knew his committee "title" (chair). However, he possibly did not understand or feel confident enough to clarify what his "role" (duties) would be as the chair.[39] This may be an appropriate topic to cover during new faculty orientation and as a reminder at the kick-off faculty meeting for each academic year.

I vividly remember (and still appreciate) that my first college department chair carefully guided me on which committees to work with during my first full year on faculty. He told me that my number one mission was to get two semesters of campus teaching under my belt. Yes, I still had to do my committee work. He took it on himself as my supervisor and mentor to guide me to and away from committees. I did not know the political and cultural landscape yet; he did.

Besides the issue of a "newbie" faculty member feeling overwhelmed, this issue highlights another issue: equitable work on committees. How does your institution make its committee appointments? Do the same people serve as chairs, serve on most of the committees, and do the lion's share of the work? Also, consider if you don't know the answers to these questions, who can help you?

• • •

***I have come to find that I'm doing most
of the work on this committee.***

• • •

APPLYING THE SEVEN RS

Before you move on to the next scenario, revisit the seven Rs. What connection(s) can you make between the material presented in this scenario and each of the seven Rs? Once you have completed that, star the principle (the one "R") that seems to be the most significant in this context and reflect on why you believe this is the most significant principle.

- Relationships
- Relevance
- Rainbows
- Resources
- Responsibility
- Reflection
- Resilience

Conference Attendance
and Participation

• • •

Organizing Question: If you attend a professional development event, in what ways should such participation benefit you, your colleagues, and your students?

Go to www.stevepiscitelli.com for supporting video.

"I DON'T GET IT," SAYS your colleague, David, as you both walk in from the parking lot one morning. "We're told to stay current in the profession. We are told to collaborate. My dean has even started asking me about what professional organizations I have leadership roles in. Not just membership, mind you, but leadership."

You nod your head. "Yeah, I heard some scuttlebutt that some of the administrators want that type of thing on our teaching evaluation."

"Well, that's an issue for another morning," says David as he holds the door open for you and you head to the coffee bar to grab a cup for the office. "Do you know there is no money, zero, zippo, nada for faculty to attend conferences? Nothing. There is nothing to help us pay for dues in professional organizations. If we do any of this, it's out of our pockets. And we haven't seen a raise in two years."

You pour a little cream into your coffee and snap a lid on the cup. "I feel the same way. But there is some good news. I heard that the college just got a federal grant, and it will pay for a limited number of faculty to attend a national conference of their choice this year. You can get up to $750."

"That's not much—but it might pay for a conference registration and maybe one night at the hotel. Thank goodness I don't eat much." David forces an ironic laugh.

"Hey, it's a start," you remind your colleague. "In order to get the money, we have to submit a one-page request that addresses the following: (1) Connection of the conference to our teaching duties and the college's mission; (2) How we will share what we learn at the conference with our colleagues here on campus; (3) What our students will do during the classes we miss; (4) The compelling reasons for attending a national conference."

"I'm not sure it's worth the hassle. But I'll give it a shot. How about we meet for lunch? Between the two of us, I know we can come up with dynamic reasons why you and I should get such a grant."

REFLECT ON THIS

* What are the compelling reasons for a faculty member to attend a professional conference?
* Does such attendance help the college? If yes, in what ways?
* If the faculty members feel strongly about attendance, should they have "some skin in the game"? That is, should they have to contribute funding to their professional growth and/or be responsible to facilitate a collegial workshop about what was learned at the conference?
* If institutional money is not available, what other resources might help in the area of faculty development?
* Can local "homegrown" opportunities meet or exceed national opportunities?
* What virtual training opportunities are available for faculty development?

* In what ways should a faculty member share his/her experiences on return to campus?

As you consider the specific reflection questions above, you may wish to give broader thought to the following:

* What VISION do you have regarding professional development and its return on investment for you, your colleagues, and your students?
* What specific CHALLENGES exist regarding this topic?
* What ACTION will you take to address the challenges and move toward your vision?
* What RESOURCES will you need?

CONSIDER THIS

Let's examine two points here: (1) What incentives exist to participate in faculty development opportunities? And (2) what happens after participation in professional development events?

INCENTIVES/DISINCENTIVES

All faculty members have a professional responsibility to stay current in their field. It comes with the calling. That being said, the institution has a responsibility in the process as well.

Do your institutional policies and climate make it easy or difficult to be engaged in professional development? The educational leaders might want to consider the roadblocks and enticements for faculty development. How do the following items impact professional opportunities and participation for the faculty on your campus?

* Ease or complexity of the application process for participation, funding, or obtaining other professional development resources

* Connection to faculty evaluation
* Institutional climate and culture
* Publication and knowledge of resources
* Networking possibilities
* Nurturing leadership
* Personal choice (perceived value)
* Personal vision and motivation
* Recognition for presentations
* Resources for opportunities
* Skillset development

ROI

What is the ROI (Return on Investment) for faculty professional development? How does the opportunity translate to faculty growth and resilience? How does it connect to student success? And how will the ROI be measured—if at all?[40]

Whether it is a local workshop or a national conference, give thought to how an off-campus development opportunity for one faculty member can be brought back to the campus to share with and enlighten colleagues.

What follows are two reflective instruments I have used with workshop participants.[41]

ROI Reflective Instrument: The Short Form
Professional Growth and Resilience
Opportunities: One and Done?

Participating in professional events marks a wonderful *start* for growth and resilience. But what is done after the event ends? What happens when the participants return to their campuses and workspaces? What do *you* do to maintain the momentum of the opportunity?

Consider submitting a simple follow-up call-to-action that outlines how information and strategies learned at the development opportunity can be applied to both professional and personal growth. Here is a simple two-step follow-up format:

Professional Applications

What specific strategies and/or information can you immediately apply to your workspace at the institution? Include the top three takeaways from your opportunity. How can these have an impact on what you do?

Personal Reflections

In what ways did you grow as a professional and an individual as a result of this experience?

ROI Reflective Instrument: The Long Form
Professional Growth and Resilience
Opportunities: One and Done?

Participating in professional events marks a wonderful *start* for growth and resilience. But what is done after the event ends? What happens when the participants return to their campuses and workspaces? What do *you* do to maintain the momentum of the opportunity?

Consider submitting a simple follow-up call-to-action that outlines how information and strategies learned at the development opportunity can be applied to both professional and personal growth. Below are a few categories to consider including.

I. Thank you!

Who (people, department, committee, or some other entity) made it possible for you to attend the event? "Made it possible" could include resources such as money, logistical support, and leave time from campus. Don't forget those coworkers who might have filled in for you during your absence.

II. PROFESSIONAL GROWTH

What specific strategies and/or information can you immediately apply to your workspace at the institution? Include the top three takeaways from your opportunity. How can these have an impact on what you do?

Did you meet any speakers, facilitators, or other participants who might have something to share on your campus?

What other insights did you gain from your participation?

How can you share knowledge and strategies gained with your colleagues?

III. PROFESSIONAL AND PERSONAL RESILIENCE

In what ways did you grow as a professional and an individual as a result of this experience?

IV. RECOMMENDATION

Would you recommend resources be committed for events like this in the future? Briefly explain your response.

• • •

Do institutional policies and climate make it easy or difficult to be engaged in professional development?

• • •

APPLYING THE SEVEN RS

Before you move on to the next scenario, revisit the seven Rs. What connection(s) can you make between the material presented in this scenario and each of the seven Rs? Once you have completed that, star the

principle (the one "R") that seems to be the most significant in this context and reflect on why you believe this is the most significant principle.

* Relationships
* Relevance
* Rainbows
* Resources
* Responsibility
* Reflection
* Resilience

Institutional Climate and Culture

• • •

Organizing Question: What impact do institutional leaders and faculty have on establishing institutional climate and culture?

Go to www.stevepiscitelli.com for supporting video.

"How will we ever gain any traction around here? Without consistent transformational leadership, we remain rudderless at this college." Professor Bo had just completed a brief presentation, at the monthly faculty senate meeting, about the importance of effective leadership for faculty and students. His college had seen a number of changes at the top administrative tier in the past eighteen months. Of the four campuses making up the college, three had interim provosts; the other had a "rookie" on the job for three months. The last college president had been forced out by the Oversight Board for the college. A new president would start in two months—but nobody, especially the faculty, had received any correspondence from the new leader.

Professor Ty, the faculty senate president, had asked some of the senior faculty members to weigh in on what toll, if any, the leadership vacuum had taken on faculty, staff, middle management, and students. The reality was that the faculty senate had minimal input on campus leadership changes. Yes, there was representation on the various screening committees, but the final decision was always made by someone in upper management and eventually approved (or vetoed) by the Board. The reason for these reports today was so that the faculty senate could compile a more comprehensive "State of the College: A Faculty Perspective." This document would detail the educational and workplace consequences due to the constant leadership change and lack of direction.

"Transformational leadership? Heck, I'd be happy with *any* leadership at this point in time," said Professor Ty. "There are so many things that we need to make decisions about at this college, but everything is on hold. And the deans are either as in the dark as us, or they fear making a move, or they just don't have the authority. Our Learning Management System (LMS) desperately needs to be updated or totally changed. The bookstore is twenty years behind the times and way overpriced for our students. We need additional faculty in many of our departments. And the technology we force our faculty to use is an embarrassment."

Professor Aleen, a faculty representative from the central campus, raised her hand to speak. "Everything you say is correct—and it is both frustrating and concerning. However, we have to get back to what we, the faculty, can do. I offer two considerations and a proposal. First, we must keep in mind that while there are challenges, we still have some excellent administrators at this college. Just like you and me, they want to make a difference for our students. I suggest we remember that and build on it by continuing to reach out to them. How can we strengthen collaboration?

"And second, we as faculty cannot change the LMS. Agreed, the bookstore needs a massive overhaul. But, again, that is totally out of faculty control. And as for technology...well, we all know of the disarray in our IT division once it also lost its associate vice president.

"My proposal—my challenge—to you, my colleagues, is this," continued Aleen. "How can we help faculty to persevere and thrive—not just grind it out and survive in the current environment? If we want leadership from above, I think we need to show leadership in the faculty ranks. I propose that we develop a practical and meaningful ten-point plan of what faculty can do to lead this institution and our students. We can be bitter or we can be better. We can cope or we can crumble."[42]

REFLECT ON THIS

* What is your evaluation of Professor Aleen's considerations and proposal?
* If you were at the meeting described in the scenario, how would you go about helping faculty to question their own biases about leadership at the college? What information do they have, and what information do they need to gather?
* What are five substantive, meaningful, and transformative actions faculty can take when they believe a leadership vacuum exists?
* Think of your leaders (past and/or present) who exemplify trans-formational leadership.[43] What did they do to empower faculty and staff on your campus? How can faculty use these same behaviors to lead their colleagues and their students?

As you consider the specific reflection questions above, you may wish to give broader thought to the following:

* What VISION do you have regarding your institutional climate and culture—and your role in establishing and maintaining such?
* What specific CHALLENGES exist regarding this topic?
* What ACTION will you take to address the challenges and move toward your vision?
* What RESOURCES will you need?

CONSIDER THIS

I have often heard colleagues say that no matter what happens "above them," what happens in the classroom makes the college what it is. The teacher-student relationship remains ground zero for action and impact.

However, just like in the scenario above, the lack of consistent college-wide leadership can create challenges for you, your colleagues, and your students. This "lack" can be due to normal turnover such as retirements, poor managerial skills, or some other combination of factors. Whatever the cause, faculty still have a job to do; a calling to pursue. While pointing fingers of blame may help to relieve some stress and strain, that rarely creates the necessary climate for cultural change.

Let's pause and consider the interplay of institutional "climate" and institutional "culture."[44]

Climate describes attitudes or actions that may have an impact on the employees and the students they serve. These can change with new leadership. The climate change, however, in and of itself does not necessarily create culture change.

In other words, people will come and go, but culture remains over time.

A new leader can come in and offer a vision of cultural change. But if the leader cannot deliver, then she will not affect cultural change. I've seen it in higher education. A new president arrives promising sweeping changes (always touted for the better in his or her perception). Two, three, or more years later and the culture remains. Why? Because the new management provides superficial climate changes.

In its simplest form, the culture refers to the ongoing behaviors of the institution that have been built over time—and will take time to change or tweak. The culture consists of the written and (maybe even more so) the unwritten rules and expectations of how "we do things around here."

Institutional climate can have an impact on institutional culture. The leaders of a college can create a climate that chills collegial relations, stymies collaboration, and chokes or removes the word "trust" from the institutional lexicon.

For instance, a new university president or vice president or dean (or, you fill in the blank) can speak of initiatives to change culture. But if the climate she or he fosters is one of intimidation and fear, chances are great that most employees will not move the ball much. They'll play it safe—and culture will not change. At the least, it will not change for the better.

Likewise, leaders can create a warm and meaningful institutional climate that nurtures a campus culture of empowerment, trust, and collegiality.

Faculty need to remember that they are not powerless in the development of institutional climate and culture. Even if your current environment is one in which the governing body and/or top management does not give you much encouragement or freedom to act independently, you can still have an impact. As a faculty member, you have control over your actions in your space. You can create the climate and culture, for instance, within your office. The way you carry yourself can have an impact on neighboring offices on your hall or in your department. You can be an agent for change within your department, on your campus, or throughout the institution. The "blame game" serves no one positively, and it may even slowly corrode collegiality.

Don't think of this as Pollyanna. Think of it as identifying what you can positively impact and then taking action. This also requires understanding the underlying assumptions that may undergird your current beliefs and actions (or inaction).

First, be aware of what the environment has to offer (opportunities and obstacles) and what you are doing (or not doing).

Second, identify assumptions you may be making about the environment and your current actions. Do this collaboratively.

Third, identify what actions you can take, what actions you may need to discontinue, and what steps may need modification.

• • •

Faculty are not powerless in the development of institutional climate and culture.

• • •

APPLYING THE SEVEN RS

Before you move on to the next scenario, revisit to the seven Rs. What connection(s) can you make between the material presented in this scenario and each of the seven Rs? Once you have completed that, star the principle (the one "R") that seems to be the most significant in this context and reflect on why you believe this is the most significant principle.

- Relationships
- Relevance
- Rainbows
- Resources
- Responsibility
- Reflection
- Resilience

SCENARIO 21

Office Hours and Appropriate Office Professionalism

• • •

Organizing Question: How can faculty most effectively use office hours?

Go to www.stevepiscitelli.com for supporting video.

CITY COLLEGE PROFESSORS MUST BE in their offices, and available for students, at least ten hours per week. The hours must be posted outside their office doors, submitted to the dean at the beginning of each semester, and distributed to the students as well (typically in the syllabus).

Professor Valentine welcomes this time. When she is in her office, her door is always open. Many times she has soft music playing. A desk-side chair is always available and free of clutter for visitors. When students visit, she turns from her computer to face the students directly. In fact, she has turned off the email alert sound so as not to interrupt any conversation she has with students or any other visitor in her office. If her office phone rings during a student visit, she lets it roll to voice mail. And her cell phone is out of sight. She never checks her cell phone for texts or any other messages or alerts while she has a visitor. "I expect my students to give our class full attention, so I need to model that expected behavior when they visit my office."

Down the hall, Professor Boutme has never particularly enjoyed his office hours. "A waste of time. Students can email me or call me if there

96

are questions." Often, he uses his designated office hours to run errands around campus. He just puts a note on the door: "Be back soon." When he is in his office, he closes the door and places paper over the window on his door for privacy. "They can knock and see if I'm in." The one side chair in his office is always piled with books and paper. When he does allow a student access to his office, he will interrupt any conversations by checking emails and answering the phone. "The students have to understand I have other students and college responsibilities. They are not unique and have to learn other people have needs as well."

REFLECT ON THIS

Critique the two professors' approaches to their required office hours. At the least, address the following:

- From your perspective, what works and what does not work?
- In the scenario above, the undergraduate professors have a requirement for ten office hours per week. A graduate school faculty member may only have to hold a couple office hours. Does the number of office hours have an impact on the quality of each hour?
- Should the dean or department chair be involved in this—or is the manner in which professors conduct office hours strictly up to them? Do you believe the institution needs to mandate office-hour expectations and behaviors?
- What are the expectations on your campus (at your institution) for faculty office hours? Consider the when, where, and how of office hours.
- Do students take advantage of your office hours? If so, share some of the techniques you use that you believe encourage them to see you.

As you consider the specific reflection questions above, you may wish to give broader thought to the following:

- What VISION do you have about office hours?
- What specific CHALLENGES exist regarding this topic?
- What ACTION will you take to address the challenges and move toward your vision?
- What RESOURCES will you need?

CONSIDER THIS

I enjoyed my office hours for a number of reasons. For instance, I could

- Work one-on-one with students.
- Establish a more validating relationship with my students.
- Answer student emails and phone calls (when I was alone in my office).
- Intervene with student groups (from the class) who might be having collaborative difficulties.
- Assist students with course selections for the coming semester. (This was not a requirement of my contract.)
- Write letters of recommendation.
- Help students find campus resources.
- Connect students with other students (more resource work).
- Plan class exercises and demonstrations.
- Evaluate student work.

Especially for my first-year and first-generation students, office hours proved to be a time to lessen (or at least, begin to lessen) anxieties about college.

With all those benefits, it still is not unusual, nationwide, for a high percentage of students to *not* take advantage of office hours.[45] Reasons could vary from embarrassment to fear to laziness to learning style to level of course competence.

From the first day, I emphasized the importance of office hours. I encouraged it at every turn. I shared the reasons (above) for office hours. I joked ("It's lonely in that office...please come and visit!"). I always kept my office door open to encourage visits.

For a few years, I included an office-visit assignment in the syllabus. Students had to establish a five-minute meeting with me in my office. The stated purpose: A time for professor and student to learn a little more about one another. The unstated purpose: Students come to see the professor's office as a welcoming location.

What can you do so that your office hours prove beneficial for your students and professionally fulfilling for yourself?

• • •

I always kept my office door open to encourage visits.

• • •

Applying The Seven Rs

Before you move on to the next scenario, revisit the seven Rs. What connection(s) can you make between the material presented in this scenario and each of the seven Rs? Once you have completed that, star the principle (the one "R") that seems to be the most significant in this context and reflect on why you believe this is the most significant principle.

* Relationships
* Relevance
* Rainbows
* Resources
* Responsibility
* Reflection
* Resilience

Collegial Collisions—Building Bridges for Collaboration

• • •

Organizing Question: What effective strategies does your institution use to build collegiality and interconnectedness?

Go to www.stevepiscitelli.com for supporting video.

"WHAT'S THIS MEAN?" ASKED PROFESSOR Stone, pushing the paper in front of her colleague. She had arrived a few minutes before the beginning of the faculty meeting and was looking at the agenda she picked up at the door as she entered the room.

"'Silos or Bridges'? Right here on the agenda."

Her colleague shrugged and gave a palms-up gesture and said, "Don't know."

The dean, Dr. Frenz, entered, and the meeting started. After he welcomed everyone and took care of some introductions and basic department housekeeping items, he turned to the agenda topic of "Silos or Bridges."

"I know it sounds cliché, but I believe our students are fortunate to learn from the finest faculty in this part of the state. No question. And they have access to more resources dedicated to their success than they will ever see again in their lives. They do have three challenges, though, with these resources. They have to know about the resources, locate them, and then use those resources for their benefit." He paused and looked around the room. He then pointed to a woman sitting in the back of the room.

"I've invited Dr. Armstrong to visit with us. As you know, she is our Dean of Student Affairs. She has a request of our fine faculty. Dr. Armstrong, would you come to the front of the room, please?"

As the Dean of Student Affairs made her way from her seat, Professor Stone leaned over and whispered to her colleague, "Geez, what are they gonna ask us to do now? I'm overloaded already."

"Thank you, Dr. Frenz, I appreciate this opportunity," began Armstrong. "And thank you for allowing me, faculty colleagues, to speak with you today. To cut to the chase, I need your help. I've been on this campus for a little over two years, and something troubles me. We seem to have two very large silos here. One silo says 'FACULTY' and the other, 'STUDENT AFFAIRS.' We don't communicate like we need to. I would like for us to collaboratively come up with a plan that will encourage meaningful collaboration between our faculty, counselors, and advisors. Ideally, I would love for representatives from Student Affairs to visit each of your classrooms within the first two weeks of the semester—just for ten or fifteen minutes—to tell the students about resources that we have for them. I think this will be a great way to begin building bridges and breaking down the silos. But we need your help. What do you think about this? How can we make it happen?"

She stopped, looked at the gathered faculty, and waited. No one spoke. No one smiled. Nothing. After what seemed like an eternity, Professor Stone raised her hand. "I appreciate your comments, but I don't have time for this. My curriculum does not allow for nonacademic stuff like this. I already provide, in the syllabus, the location of the Student Affairs Center. If the students can't take a little initiative to find these resources on their own, then shame on them."

A few faculty nodded in agreement. Stony silence followed.

Reflect on This

Imagine this: You have been approached by your dean to chair an institution-wide committee that will evaluate whether or not silos actually exist on campus. He wants an assessment of what you and your colleagues do at your institution to increase the opportunities for collaboration. He told you recently, "If we are to help students connect with resources, then we need to know about those resources as well. We all need a working knowledge of all the moving parts of this institution."

If you and your committee members find that cooperation is strained, you will be expected to make recommendations to foster collaboration. Where you find collaboration already existing, you will demonstrate how that collaboration shows itself, and you will make recommendations to continue and augment these bright spots.

Your dean has asked you to give recommendations on the following:

• Who should serve on this committee with you? What departments or areas need to be represented?
• Will you have student representation on the committee? Why or why not?
• How will you determine if there is collaboration or not? And how can you determine the current degree of collaboration?
• For your institution, identify three "bright spots" that currently exist. That is, where do you find shining examples of colleagues reaching beyond their comfort zones and "space" to work with and understand the operations and strengths of a department or area other than their own?
• Identify three "not-so-bright spots" that currently exist. That is, what challenges exist that may or do hinder collaboration? What can be done in these cases?

As you consider the specific reflection questions above, you may wish to give broader thought to the following:

• What VISION do you have regarding collaborations with other departments, programs, and colleagues at your institution?
• What specific CHALLENGES exist regarding this topic?
• What ACTION will you take to address the challenges and move toward your vision?
• What RESOURCES will you need?

CONSIDER THIS

When Tony Hsieh of Zappos moved his headquarters to Las Vegas, he actually reduced the number of open entrances and exits to and from his office building. He wanted to increase the opportunities for people to bump into one another, or as he said, "maximize collisions and accelerate serendipity."[46]

Reflect on that for a moment. We have to connect (or collide) before we can collaborate. Some campus cultures do this effortlessly. Whether due to transformative leadership or the personalities and drive of the staff, cross-discipline conversations and interdepartmental cooperation have become the norm. Silos do not exist; bridges do.

Other institutions are plagued by "us vs. them" attitudes and actions. For instance, you may have encountered metaphorical walls (that create actual barriers to communication) between such entities as:

* Faculty—Student Affairs (Services)
* Faculty—Administration
* Faculty Discipline—Another Faculty Discipline
* Student Services—Administration
* Administration—Support Staff (office)
* Faculty—Support Staff (office)
* Custodians—All others
* Other—Another

Finally, regardless of the level of collaboration on your campus, let's engage in a bit of imagery.[†††] Consider that when you look at your job description, *collaboration* is written into it. It is an expectation. Now, close your eyes and do the following:

[†††] Special thanks to Karen Armstrong, Career Counselor at Penn State University, for the inspiration—and a lot of the wording—for this imagery section. Karen and I collaborated extensively—she as a counselor and me as a faculty member—when we both worked at Florida State College at Jacksonville (Downtown Campus). For one collaborative example, see our video on YouTube titled "What Would You Do? A Critical Thinking Exercise," September 5, 2013, https://youtu.be/X5YegUnQrTs.

- Imagine faculty working together—no success or "glory" without collaboration. What would this look like on your campus?
- Imagine faculty and student affairs staff collaborating closely in the development of new student orientation or recruitment workshops. How would that look?
- What if student affairs proctored faculty exams and faculty were involved with advising in their programs of study? What would look different on your campus?
- Finally, what benefits could come to your campus culture if faculty were invited (and attended) student affairs meetings, and counselors and advisors were invited (and attended) faculty meetings?

Whatever or wherever the separation occurs, it can stymie collaboration. Depending on the thickness and height of the silo walls, they may sabotage partnerships, problem solving, and innovation.

• • •

We have to connect before we can collaborate. Some campus cultures do this effortlessly. Others struggle.

• • •

APPLYING THE SEVEN RS

Before you move on to the next scenario, revisit the seven Rs. What connection(s) can you make between the material presented in this scenario and each of the seven Rs? Once you have completed that, star the principle (the one "R") that seems to be the most significant in this context and reflect on why you believe this is the most significant principle.

- Relationships
- Relevance
- Rainbows
- Resources
- Responsibility
- Reflection
- Resilience

Differing Perceptions on Teaching Efficacy

• • •

Organizing Question: What factors affect teaching efficacy?

Go to www.stevepiscitelli.com for supporting video.

FACULTY ENTERED THE ROOM FOR their kick-off of the semester faculty meeting. The dean welcomed each faculty member with a warm smile and greeting as they came into the room. He was authentic and connected with each faculty member as if he or she were the only person in the room.

The first thing the faculty noticed (after the warm reception) was the setup of the room. They had been using this same classroom for faculty meetings for the last three years. It comfortably fit everyone and allowed for a degree of intimacy and ease of communication. Today the tables had been removed and chairs were set up in two large circles—one circle on either side of the room. On the wall closest to each circle was a piece of flip chart paper.

One side of the room said, "The bottom line for teaching and learning is what the student brings into the classroom. The professor cannot do much if the student is not motivated."

On the other side, the paper read, "With few exceptions and with my diligent effort, I can reach even the most challenging student."

The dean instructed his faculty to take a seat. "I realize few people will agree totally with each statement. For our purposes today, I would like for you to sit nearest the sign that you believe captures what you have experienced, for the most part, in your teaching career."

Matt, a math professor with a sense of humor, moved his seat to the middle space between the two circles. He sat there and smiled.

With that, the faculty chose their seats, and the meeting began.

REFLECT ON THIS

* Reflect on when you were a student. Did you find your professors' sense of efficacy motivating and important to your learning? Briefly explain.
* Where would you sit in this meeting—and for what reasons?
* Does a teacher's confidence in his or her ability to "reach" the students matter?
* What other teacher habits or traits do you believe are critical when it comes to teacher efficacy?
* In what ways does a teacher's view of teaching efficacy affect his or her teaching? Be specific.
* In what ways do teacher views of teaching efficacy affect student learning? Be specific.
* How important is a faculty mentoring program in developing teaching efficacy?
* Can teaching efficacy be "lost" or diminished over the years?
* How do you and your colleagues develop a sense of teaching efficacy?
* In what ways can teaching efficacy be affected by the school or campus climate and culture?

As you consider the specific reflection questions above, you may wish to give broader thought to the following:

* What VISION do you have regarding the power you have to make a difference in the lives of your students?
* What specific CHALLENGES exist regarding this topic?
* What ACTION will you take to address the challenges and move toward your vision?
* What RESOURCES will you need?

CONSIDER THIS

Teacher efficacy, in short, is the teacher's belief that he or she can impact student learning. Some teachers may believe that teachers (in general) can affect student learning, *but* they may not have the confidence that *they* can do it. From elementary school teachers to tenured college professors, a sense of efficacy can be tied to factors such as past success, general sense of resilience, mentoring relationships, feedback from colleagues and students, length of teaching experience, administrative support, and the climate and culture of the institution.[47]

Take time to do the following:

* Think of the colleagues in your department. Focus on one who truly exemplifies teaching efficacy. List three things this faculty colleague does in his or her teaching that has had an impact on teaching and learning. Why do you think he or she is so efficacious?
* On a scale of 0 (I don't believe teachers can make a difference in learning if the student is not motivated) to 10 (The teacher is the motivator and the reason for learning), where do you stand? Please do not use the number 5. Briefly support your ranking.

• • •

Teacher efficacy reflects the teacher's belief that
he or she can impact student learning.

• • •

Applying The Seven Rs

Before you move on to the next scenario, revisit the seven Rs. What connection(s) can you make between the material presented in this scenario and each of the seven Rs? Once you have completed that, star the principle (the one "R") that seems to be the most significant in this context and reflect on why you believe this is the most significant principle.

* Relationships
* Relevance
* Rainbows
* Resources
* Responsibility
* Reflection
* Resilience

SCENARIO 24

Empathic Engagement with Students

• • •

Organizing Question: Does the act of teaching include a space for empathic engagement with students?

Go to www.stevepiscitelli.com for supporting video.

DEAN LINCOLN AND ONE OF his veteran faculty, Professor Stanton, are meeting today to discuss last week's classroom observation and the most-recent student evaluations of faculty. The dean has been in the current position for one year. Professor Stanton has been at this campus for going on twenty-five years, all of them in the history department. He is a recognized expert in his field and has widely published on the Civil War era.

"Professor, thank you for meeting with me today. I first want to say that I thoroughly enjoyed my visit to your class last week. Your lecture taught me things I never knew about military tactics."

"Well, dean, you know that is a passion of mine. It all started with my dissertation nearly thirty years ago. Thank you for your feedback."

"I have additional observations and questions that I would like to get your feedback about." The dean referred to the notes he had typed on his tablet during the class visit.

"You lectured for the entire seventy-five minutes I was in your class. I don't remember that you asked the students any questions about the content. What are your thoughts about student engagement during a class session? How do you know when the students 'get it'—that is, get your main point? And what are your thoughts about student questions during your lectures?"

The dean had noted that during the lecture, a couple students did raise their hands, but the professor never engaged or recognized them.

The professor was quick to answer. He had been through these conversations with past deans.

"I find out if they 'got it,'" he said, raising his hands to make air quotes, "when I test them on it. The reason I don't engage them in questions is that over the years I have found that they don't know how to answer any question other than recall questions. I have too much to cover to waste time with factual recall questions. They can take notes, get notes from a classmate, read the textbook, or search the Internet. No need to recognize the students. This isn't Q and A. It's a lecture survey course. And, anyway, I am always available during office hours for students. I welcome and enjoy when they stop by!"

The dean opened a folder on his desk. "I think I'm seeing some connections to your most previous evaluation. You scored at the top of the scale on 'Knows the Content' and, also, on 'Returns Assignments Expeditiously.' Thank you for that. And you scored at or near the bottom of these areas:

- Is Understanding and Compassionate
- Is Willing to Help and Explain Content
- Is Interesting and Interactive in Class
- Listens to Student Concerns

"What are your thoughts about these evaluation variations?"

"Listen," said Professor Stanton, "they have lives just like you and me. If I have a bad hair day at home, don't you still expect me to show up and do my job? Same with them. I'm not a counselor. I'm not an entertainer. I'm not their daddy. I think they need to get used to that sooner than later. This college pays me to teach history, not to identify and understand their emotions and feelings. I'd never get through the content if all we did is make allowances for their inquiries and hardships—perceived or real."

REFLECT ON THIS

- Is part of a teacher's job to be empathic—take or understand the perspective of the student?
- Look at the areas (noted above) that Professor Stanton scored low on his evaluation. Are these meaningful or relevant measures for the teaching and learning process? How do you know they are or are not relevant and meaningful?
- Should there be engagement in the classroom to gauge student comprehension—or is that what the summative tests are for?
- Briefly describe why you would or would not want to be a student in Professor Stanton's class.
- Briefly describe why you would or would not want a family member to be a student in Professor Stanton's class.

As you consider the specific reflection questions above, you may wish to give broader thought to the following:

- What VISION do you have regarding empathic teaching?
- What specific CHALLENGES exist regarding this topic?
- What ACTION will you take to address the challenges and move toward your vision?
- What RESOURCES will you need?

CONSIDER THIS

This scenario touches on so many pertinent issues: student evaluations of faculty, supervisory relationships, teaching strategies, a teacher's role or roles, mentoring, and empathy. You could go in a number of directions with this. Let's examine one: empathy.

Daniel Goleman speaks about three types of empathy.[48] Strong leaders and top performing teams, according to Goleman, have all three. As you read the three items below, consider the connection to you as a classroom instructor.

1. Cognitive empathy. With this we can say to someone, "I know what you are feeling. I can see things from your perspective." We communicate and connect.
2. Emotional empathy. Goleman said that this form of empathic connection allows us to sense what another person is feeling. "I feel your distress."
3. Empathic concern. Here we go beyond "feeling" another's hurt. We want to help the person navigate the hurt. It becomes the basis for our concern. Transformational leaders give effective feedback and help people and teams grow.[49]

So, is there a connection between teaching and empathy? If so, in what ways? Or, is Professor Stanton (scenario above) correct when he states, "This college pays me to teach content. Not to identify and understand their emotions and feelings. I'd never get through the content if all we did is make allowances for their inquiries and hardships—perceived or real"?

• • •

Strong leaders and top performing teams
have three types of empathy.

• • •

APPLYING THE SEVEN RS

Before you move on to the next scenario, revisit the seven Rs. What connection(s) can you make between the material presented in this scenario and each of the seven Rs? Once you have completed that, star the

principle (the one "R") that seems to be the most significant in this context and reflect on why you believe this is the most significant principle.

* Relationships
* Relevance
* Rainbows
* Resources
* Responsibility
* Reflection
* Resilience

No Cell Phones During Our Meetings

• • •

Organizing Question: Is technology undermining our ability to engage in meaningful and empathetic conversations and collaborations?

Go to www.stevepiscitelli.com for supporting video.

"HEY, JIM, DID YOU SEE that email the dean just sent?" asked Nancy as she poked her head into her colleague's office. "Please tell me I'm missing something. Or has she reverted back to the 1980s?"

"Yeah, I just read it. I think I understand where the dean is coming from, but then again, I'm not sure." Jim searched his email inbox and found the email Nancy had referenced. "It appears she feels people are no longer 'totally in' our faculty meetings. Everyone either has their heads buried in a tablet, laptop, or cell phone rather than fully engaging the meeting."

"Well, we might be 'totally in' those meetings if they held any substance," countered Nancy. "If we taught the way she conducts meetings, I can only imagine what our student evaluations would be like. And anyway, I can't speak for others, but I have a very agile and active mind. I can do more than one thing at once. I wonder if she has ever heard of multitasking."

"It looks like starting with our Wednesday meeting this week that all technology is banned from the meeting room. If it is in the room, it has to be off. And she is asking us not to step out of the room to make phone calls or text," Jim stated as he read the email out loud. "Her final section states,

I realize this will not be a popular decision, and we might just have to agree to disagree about whether we can multitask or not. On a very basic level, when you, me, or anyone else is attending to our email, texts, or social-media sites, the message we send to everyone in the room is that they don't matter to you. While I'm not a troglodyte, I do believe this constant attention to the 'out there world' is killing our conversations and any chance of holding meaningful empathetic dialogue about issues that matter. We expect respect from our students. We need to hold the same standard for ourselves."

Nancy shook her head. "I don't like it and will say so Wednesday. Her problem is that she is stuck in a pre-Internet mind-set. She is not being respectful of our desires and needs. Who do these *faculty* meetings belong to anyway?"

REFLECT ON THIS

* What is the situation in your faculty meetings? Are people "on" technology?
* List three reasons that support the dean's decision in this scenario and three reasons that do not support the dean's decision.
* What about the statement "We expect respect from our students. We need to hold the same standard for ourselves"? Do you agree? Are there different levels of respect?
* Nancy alludes to a generational divide. To what extent does this contribute to the situation in this scenario?
* What about colleagues who would like to use their tablets for taking notes at the meeting? Should this be allowed?
* Other than the two extremes of no technology allowed or use whatever you have whenever you want, is there a middle ground on this issue?

As you consider the specific reflection questions above, you may wish to give broader thought to the following:

* What VISION do you have regarding technology and distractions during professional gatherings?
* What specific CHALLENGES exist regarding this topic?
* What ACTION will you take to address the challenges and move toward your vision?
* What RESOURCES will you need?

CONSIDER THIS

Whether we talk about the switch-tasking, technologically induced isolation, or decreasing attention spans, we have become a society (world) tethered to our technological devices. Just pay attention to those you pass on your walk from the campus parking lot, through the lobby, past the coffee shop, and to your classroom. How many cell phones do you see in hand at the ready for use or in use with earbuds firmly in place?

One perspective (beyond collaborative respect), I presented to my students involved potential safety issues. Is it safe to have earbuds ensconced in one's ears, music playing, and then lean into the car trunk to gather books or walk through the parking lot toward the classroom oblivious to your surroundings? Perhaps you could share and discuss some research as well. For instance,

* John Medina, in his book *Brain Rules*, examines the multitasking myth.[50] What we really do is switch task (or back task). And when we do switch tasks, we actually become less efficient with the task in front of us.
* Sherry Turkle, in her book *Alone Together*, fears that technology actually makes us more isolated rather than more connected.

Levine and Dean reference the same phenomenon in their book *Generation on a Tightrope.*[51]

* Nicholas Carr, author of *The Shallows: What the Internet Is Doing to Our Brains,* writes that technological advances come with opportunity costs—one being our increasing inability to pay attention and reflect for an extended period of time.[52]

So, does any of this matter? Or are we in a never-ending collective monologue where each group tenaciously holds on to the confirmation biases and narrow framing of its position?

Would it be any different if, instead of a cell phone or tablet, the person you were (supposedly) conversing with kept his eyes continuously glued to a book, magazine, or newspaper while you spoke, never making eye contact? Should the dean have the freedom to structure her meetings as she deems most appropriate?

Or have the rules of civility changed to a degree that demands our conversational expectations need to change as well?

• • •

Constant attention to the "out there world" is killing our conversations and any chance of holding meaningful empathetic dialogue about issues that matter.

• • •

APPLYING THE SEVEN RS

Before you move on to the next scenario, revisit the seven Rs. What connection(s) can you make between the material presented in this scenario and each of the seven Rs? Once you have completed that, star the principle (the one "R") that seems to be the most significant in this context and reflect on why you believe this is the most significant principle.

* Relationships
* Relevance
* Rainbows
* Resources
* Responsibility
* Reflection
* Resilience

Recovering from a "Bad" Class Session

• • •

Organizing Question: What can an instructor do after a less-than-effective class meeting?

Go to www.stevepiscitelli.com for supporting video.

PROFESSOR JEFFERSON KNOCKED ON PROFESSOR Adams's office door. "Got a minute, John?"

Adams turned from his computer and waved his colleague in. "Sure, sure. Take a seat, Tom. What's up?"

"I'm frustrated. Need your feedback. Here's the situation." As Jefferson slid into the chair, he continued. "I was really excited for class today. The topic, analyzing the Declaration of Independence, always brings a lot of conversation. Just about all of my students have never really looked at the words of that document. So I guide them through a discussion of the wording—almost line by line. We focus on key words and phrases." Jefferson leaned forward in his chair as he shared his lesson with his colleague.

"Sounds intriguing to me. But do you really expect a bunch of nonmajors to really get into that conversation?" Adams sat back in his chair, took a sip of his coffee, and raised an eyebrow.

"Yes, I do! And over the semesters, they always have. I consider myself a fairly capable facilitator and a provocative questioner. So, I feel this is my strong suit."

"OK. What was the problem? Why are you frustrated?"

"Well, today, when we got to the phrase 'All men are created equal' and started to dissect the meaning, all hell broke loose. It turned into a racial argument that quickly spun out of control. The next thing I knew, two of my younger students, sitting on opposite sides of the room, started throwing slurs at one another and charged each other. I attempted to stop them by stepping in between them. Next thing I knew, I was tossed over the desk, my notes went flying. Students were jumping on tables. A few helped me up. A number of the cooler-headed students separated the combatants before any punches were thrown. Security was summoned. And just as quickly as it started, it ended."

Adams's eyes were wide open. "Damn. You do know how to get them involved, Tom!" He attempted a smile.

"Frankly, I'm embarrassed," said a sullen Jefferson as he sank into his chair. "I have no idea how to rebound from this when the next class starts. Do I acknowledge it, ignore it, or make a joke about it? Do I just revert to lectures and forget about engaging conversations and hot-button issues? Do I go boring instead of provocative?"

REFLECT ON THIS

- What is your advice to Professor Jefferson? How should he handle the next class meeting?
- Are there certain trigger words (see Scenario 27) or topics that should never be addressed in class? If so, is "All men are created equal" one of those topics?
- Should a teacher stay away from the provocative questions in favor of the safe and "vanilla" topics?
- Should a classroom reflect society at large, a society in which students will have to confront and deal (effectively) with controversial topics and opposing viewpoints?
- If what happened to Professor Jefferson happened to you, would you have shared it with a colleague as Jefferson does in this scenario?

Or would you have kept it to yourself either out of shame, pride, or the need to remain private in your thoughts?

As you consider the specific reflection questions above, you may wish to give broader thought to the following:

* What VISION do you have when it comes to reflecting on effective and less-than-effective class sessions you have with your students?
* What specific CHALLENGES exist regarding this topic?
* What ACTION will you take to address the challenges and move toward your vision?
* What RESOURCES will you need?

CONSIDER THIS

Before you do an eye roll about the above scenario, let me tell you this: It really happened in one class. And the professor in question was not Tom Jefferson—it was me. It is one of the "critical incidents" of my career.

Stephen Brookfield describes a critical incident as an event that for some reason we vividly recall.[53] I can tell you that, for sure, this event was unplanned, unanticipated, and I vividly remember it!

I was a bit rattled to say the least. A few students did help me to my feet and gathered up my notes. They seemed to be more concerned about me than anything else. The incident happened at the end of the class period for the day. After I ascertained that everyone in the room was OK and that security had taken control of the matter, the students left for the day.

Later that day, both of the students involved in the altercation came to my office (separately) to apologize for what happened. Both were suspended from the campus for the rest of the semester (as best as I remember, this happened around 2001). The next time I met with the class, I brought the elephant in the corner to the center of the room. I explained my disappointment in how the incident evolved. We discussed the importance of open and, at times, controversial discussions. If we could not do that on a college campus, then how could we expect for it to happen in society in general? I told them I hoped we could continue to have such conversations, and they agreed.

The event always stayed with me. It reminded me that while it can be effective to facilitate a provocative discussion, I needed to be aware (more aware) of who was in the room. This was in an era before I had heard about "trigger words." But I came to more of a realization that "All men are created equal" was a trigger phrase for some. While "trigger" was not in my lexicon then, I explained to the students (and myself as I reflected) that an effective facilitator needs to be able to broach controversial or provocative topics, engage the audience in meaningful conversation (not vanilla pabulum), and help the students understand there are other views that we may not like. It became an appropriate time to speak about civility.

Every semester thereafter, when I introduced my Declaration of Independence lesson, I always told the class about the critical incident above. It became an enduring teaching and learning moment.

A side note: An added dimension exists in today's classroom that the teacher might want to consider in such situations. At the beginning of the twenty-first century, the ability to immediately post videos to a social-media platform did not exist as it does today. Video uploads to social-media were futuristic thoughts at best. Does the social-media medium—and the ability for an event to go viral and live on long after it happened—create a different texture for handling such an incident today?

One more note: Are you familiar with your campus policies about classroom disruptions? What would you need to do if a situation (like in this scenario) happened in your classroom?

• • •

An effective facilitator needs skill to broach provocative topics and engage the audience in meaningful conversation.

• • •

Applying The Seven Rs

Before you move on to the next scenario, revisit the seven Rs. What connection(s) can you make between the material presented in this scenario and each of the seven Rs? Once you have completed that, star the principle (the one "R") that seems to be the most significant in this context and reflect on why you believe this is the most significant principle.

* Relationships
* Relevance
* Rainbows
* Resources
* Responsibility
* Reflection
* Resilience

SCENARIO 27

Trigger Warnings

• • •

Organizing Question: Should a "rating" (similar to a movie) be applied to each syllabus, each class, every discussion topic, and/or college in general?

Go to www.stevepiscitelli.com for supporting video.

THE FACULTY SENATE AGENDA HAD two simple words listed under the "For Discussion" part of the meeting: "Trigger Warnings." The senate president knew they would engender quite a bit of heated discussion. In fact, one of his senate colleagues wryly noted that perhaps the words "trigger warnings" should themselves be subject to a "trigger warning."[54]

The agenda also held this brief description:

> *Trigger Warnings are cautionary flags (red lights) that professors at various institutions have been asked to post (or consider posting) in their syllabi if there might be words, texts, discussions or the like that might offend someone in the classroom. In other words, if a discussion or reading might trigger a recollection of a past personal trauma in a student, the student should be given warning. Discussions have to be safe. Anything that could be considered a "microaggression" (a well-intentioned comment or view that could be considered insulting or derogatory to another person) has to be avoided at all costs.[55]*

Is there "a right not to be offended" by a topic, opinion, or line of questioning in the teaching and learning environment?

The senate meeting drew a standing room only crowd of faculty on this particular day to speak on the topic. The first professor, opposed to any kind of trigger warnings, closed his presentation with the following series of questions:

"Should war be skirted as a classroom topic of deep conversation because it might offend or cause uneasiness? Would the following topics qualify for trigger warnings because students might associate the topic with uncomfortable feelings or experiences from their past?

- Binge drinking
- Date rape
- Domestic violence
- Failure
- Financial literacy and indebtedness
- Gender issues
- Goal achieving
- Learning disabilities
- Mental illness
- Obesity
- Political disagreements
- Prenatal care
- Race
- Religious beliefs
- Slavery
- Smoking
- Suicide
- Tobacco use
- The Confederate flag
- The Holocaust
- Vulnerability
- War

"If someone had a traumatic memory associated with any of those, does the classroom discussion have to cease or be sanitized? A teacher might not know that she has triggered some trauma. I guess, anything can be construed as potentially traumatic to someone in the room.

"If we move to trigger warnings, will teachers be able to encourage students to critically think about controversial or sensitive issues? If we allow students to 'opt-out' of discussions, will they be able to avoid confronting confounding information that might make them question their beliefs?

"What does this do to the First Amendment and a teacher's right (and professional duty) to construct and deliver meaningful lessons? Is it the thought police? Is this censorship by another word? Is it an example of a litigation-averse preemptive counterattack?"

The professor closed his notes and took his seat.

Reflect on This

- List three reasons that support the use of trigger warnings.
- List three reasons that would show the folly of trigger warnings.
- Is there a middle ground? What other questions should we be asking regarding this topic?
- What do you see as the benefits and challenges of the "opt-out" of discussion option for students?
- Are colleges and universities, as one writer posited, guilty of the "infantilization of the American undergraduate"?[56]

As you consider the specific reflection questions above, you may wish to give broader thought to the following:

- What VISION do you have regarding teaching, learning, and trigger warnings?
- What specific CHALLENGES exist regarding this topic?

- What ACTION will you take to address the challenges and move toward your vision?
- What RESOURCES will you need?

Consider This

Should higher education come with a warning such as the following?

Warning: While attending this college (university), you may be exposed to views you don't agree with and/or that might make you feel uncomfortable and/or that you would rather not discuss.
Feel free to opt-out as you see fit.

As our professor in the scenario did, let me leave you with more questions than answers:

- Does your institution have a mechanism to discuss issues of (perceived or real) microaggressions?[57]
- Do you have a supportive collegial network to help you identify and navigate potential minefields?
- If students raise the red flag of microaggression, does a similar process exist for faculty (and support staff and administrative personnel) who believe they have been the victims of microaggression? Should faculty meeting agendas come, for instance, with trigger warnings?

• • •

If we move to trigger warnings, will teachers be able to encourage students to critically think about controversial or sensitive issues?

• • •

APPLYING THE SEVEN RS

Before you move on to the next scenario, revisit the seven Rs. What connection(s) can you make between the material presented in this scenario and each of the seven Rs? Once you have completed that, star the principle (the one "R") that seems to be the most significant in this context and reflect on why you believe this is the most significant principle.

* Relationships
* Relevance
* Rainbows
* Resources
* Responsibility
* Reflection
* Resilience

Appropriate Accommodations

• • •

Organizing Question: How does a classroom instructor go about developing meaningful, authentic, and empathic relationships with students with disabilities?

Go to www.stevepiscitelli.com for supporting video.

"I THINK I HAVE SHELDON Cooper in my biology class." Professor Perryani referenced the main character of a popular television sitcom as he described a student in his class to a campus counselor.‡‡‡

"This student, Vincent, seems to have an absolute inability to understand or appreciate other students. It's as if he believes he's the only one in the room. At times I have used sarcasm in class to get a particular point across or just to inject a bit of humor, and he just does not get it. He takes everything literally. Even when I or the students use facial expressions to indicate sarcasm, he doesn't seem to read those expressions."

The counselor nodded his head as he took a piece of paper on which the professor had written the student's full name and college ID number. "Have you had a conversation with Vincent during office hours?"

"Well, that's another issue. When I asked him, privately after class one day, if he had time to chat, he got very anxious. He started telling me about his schedule and how he could not deviate from it. So, I assumed he had to get to work or had some sort of appointment. I offered another day

---

‡‡‡ The television show is *The Big Bang Theory* on the CBS network at this writing.

and time. He said, and this floored me, 'Oh, professor, I don't have a job. But I have a specific time each day to do certain things. Class is scheduled to end at twelve noon and I have to be in the cafeteria by 12:10 p.m. to order my cheeseburger—cooked medium, with only mustard. I then go to the drink counter to get my twenty-four-ounce slushy—has to be grape. There is a certain seat I sit at each day, by the window in the corner. If it is occupied, I will stand close by until the person leaves...' And," said the professor, "Vincent will go on and on and on relating the smallest details. He is the most annoying student I have had in a long time. But all of that is not as bad as what he does when he disagrees with someone. He will tell classmates they just don't understand because they don't know as much as him. He always says, 'I've looked into this, so I know.' *And* he is always offering his very detailed opinions. He doesn't understand that no one really cares about these minute details."

"What's your next step?" the counselor asked as he pecked at his keyboard.

"That's why I'm here with you. I'm totally lost. Vincent is not a bad kid at all. I have a sense that he just does not understand what he is doing and how it is perceived by those around him. He's just so different, at least to me. I'm out of my bag of tricks. It's even gotten to the point that students don't wish to work with him in group settings in or out of class. The last straw for me was today in class. I told the class we would need to move to another room for the next few class meetings, as the IT staff needed to do some equipment upgrades in our classroom. He exploded saying that was unacceptable as 'This is my classroom; I don't see why I need to change rooms!' He even said I was being unreasonable. Right there in a classroom full of students. It was not only frustrating but, frankly, very insulting."

The counselor turned back to the professor from his computer screen. "Well, I do not see that he has been approved for or even requested any accommodations."

"Well, then, what do we do?" Professor Perryani sunk into his chair, waiting for a response from his student services colleague. "Does he even belong here at this college?"

REFLECT ON THIS

- List what you consider to be the bright spots in this scenario. That is, do you see anything that is positive and on which the professor and counselor can build?
- What do you think would be the most effective strategy (for teacher, counselor, and student) at this point?
- What do you think would be the least effective strategy (for teacher, counselor, and student) at this point?
- On your campus, who handles situations such as this?
- How does FERPA address situations such as this?
- How would you ask the student about his challenges in the classroom? Do you know what you can or cannot say or ask?
- Who else might be able to help the classroom teacher and student?
- Respond to the professor's question: "Does he even belong here at this college?"

As you consider the specific reflection questions above, you may wish to give broader thought to the following:

- What VISION do you have regarding helping students with disabilities thrive in your class?
- What specific CHALLENGES exist regarding this topic?
- What ACTION will you take to address the challenges and move toward your vision?
- What RESOURCES will you need?

CONSIDER THIS

Faculty do not get to screen who enrolls in their classes. They get an attendance list and the students enter the classroom. And when they enter, the teacher's job is to connect with those students. Remember, one of the key principles for life success (and this book) is that of establishing meaningful and authentic relationships. With some students, that may be a challenge.

Besides the underlying and driving importance of treating our human interactions with respect and civility, we are also guided by appropriate laws. While you (and most of your teaching colleagues) may *not* have been trained as counselors or therapists, there are a few basic things you can do to help your students with disabilities navigate their college journey.

- Know the campus and institutional resources available to your students. How can you direct your students to the counselors and advisors who can help them? Obviously, you can't guide your students to resources if you don't know they exist.

- As our professor in the scenario above did, reach out to the student in a nonthreatening manner that respects his or her privacy. Can you establish, or begin to establish, a relationship of trust? Again, consider what you can or cannot say to or about students.

- Does the student already have accommodations in place? This is where a relationship with your student affairs colleagues can be beneficial.

- Can you reach out to faculty colleagues who have worked with this student in the past? Perhaps they will have suggestions for you.

- Educate yourself as much as possible with practical information. I know that my counselor colleagues guided me in many situations. They helped me and my colleagues avoid taking well-meaning but ill-advised steps that we thought could help a student.

- A scenario as the one above may even open up conversations about accommodations in general. For instance, perhaps you want to talk about whether accommodations give unfair advantages to the student who needs them (i.e., extra time on assignments, testing in a quiet environment, access to material ahead of time). Are these requirements fair? Why or why not? Do colleagues feel like they are being given "additional duties and responsibilities" (like audio or video recording a lesson or wearing a microphone)? Yes, the accommodations may be dictated to the faculty member, but if the faculty member is harboring such concerns, it might prove useful to put those concerns on the table and talk about them.

Above all, think partnership with all involved: student, faculty, counselor, and resources. How can you carry out this conversation on your campus? In what ways can appropriate accommodations and training be offered for the benefit of the student and classroom instructor?

● ● ●

Besides the underlying and driving importance of treating our human interactions with respect and civility, we are also guided by appropriate laws.

● ● ●

Applying The Seven Rs

Before you move on to the next scenario, revisit the seven Rs. What connection(s) can you make between the material presented in this scenario and each of the seven Rs? Once you have completed that, star the principle (the one "R") that seems to be the most significant in this context and reflect on why you believe this is the most significant principle.

* Relationships
* Relevance
* Rainbows
* Resources
* Responsibility
* Reflection
* Resilience

Do Faculty Understand the Role of Administrators?

• • •

Organizing Question: What does your institution do (and what else could it do) to help faculty understand the demands, expectations, and challenges that administrators face on a day-to-day basis?

Go to www.stevepiscitelli.com for supporting video.

TAD FITZGERALD, THE DEAN OF Liberal Arts on his campus, sat with his colleague Wesley Wiscot, the associate dean. It was their usual Monday-morning meeting. As they each sipped on a cup of coffee, they reviewed the agenda for the week.

"I'm not looking forward to our Wednesday faculty meeting," offered Wesley as he fingered the agenda in his hand. "You and I put a lot of thought into these meetings, and all we ever get are stares and glares from the faculty. They take everything so freaking personally. Like our sole job is to make their lives miserable. I tell you, Tad, those meetings are the longest ninety minutes of my life. I know we have some very good faculty, but there are a few in there who, pardon me, seem to simply resent anything we propose. It's tiring."

Tad nodded to his colleague. He, too, understood the frustration. He had been the dean for the past eighteen months. While he had seen some improvement in the meetings, he still found a bit of tension existed. "You know," he said as he put down his coffee cup, "I have seen a slight softening of attitudes. But we have ways to go. I really don't think it's the meetings as much as the overall relationship between faculty and administration. You and I are fairly new to the institution, but I know from talking with faculty and other administrators that there is a long history of mistrust here between the classroom instructors and the management of the university."

"You're right," said Wesley. "But you and I have bent over backward to build trust. We are very visible, not intrusive, and definitely not some faceless entities sending out email blasts. We have attempted to have off-campus get-togethers in the afternoon to build collegiality. We have secured more funding for professional development than they have seen on this campus in the last decade. I'm not sure they really understand—or care—about the battles we fight in the administrative food chain on their behalf every day."

Tad thought for a moment and then wrote the word TRUST at the top of a piece of paper. "Our job," he offered, "is to continue to build that trust. I believe we have started that, and we have some great faculty who get it. But we have not been clear—or maybe, transparent enough—about our goals for closer collegial collaborations. If, as you say, the faculty really don't understand what we do, then I believe our job is to help them understand that. We attempt to understand their roles by visiting their classroom, stopping by their offices, and visiting with them in the cafeteria. But what have we done to make it easier for them to understand the administrative perspective? That is our task. And I think I have a few ideas that just might get the ball rolling."

With that, Tad started to list and explain to Wesley the components of his nascent plan.

Reflect on This

* If you were the dean, what would be your plan to help faculty understand what administrators do?

- Would it be helpful to have a way for faculty to "shadow" their deans?
- Is this distrust simply part of the territory of faculty-administrative relationships—with nothing that can be done to lessen the tensions?
- What would you suggest to your dean as a way to build trust?
- Think of the effective leaders for whom you have worked. What did they do well to be or to become effective?
- Think of the ineffective leaders for whom you have worked. What resulted from their actions or inactions?

As you consider the specific reflection questions above, you may wish to give broader thought to the following:

- What VISION do you have regarding establishing effective faculty-administration collegial working relationships?
- What specific CHALLENGES exist regarding this topic?
- What ACTION will you take to address the challenges and move toward your vision?
- What RESOURCES will you need?

CONSIDER THIS

I have often heard faculty question whether or not administrators really understand what occurs each day in the classrooms. (And, truth be told, I occasionally offered up similar questions.) At times there seem to be disconnections for sure.

The intent of this scenario is to turn the perspective for a moment. Rather than ask, "Don't those administrators have a clue about what faculty do each day?" I am proposing we take the perspective of Associate Dean Wiscot in the scenario above when he states, "I'm not sure faculty really understand—or care—about the battles we fight in the administrative food chain on their behalf every day."

If faculty want fruitful conversations, it may be helpful to start questioning faculty assumptions and seeking to understand the administrative viewpoint.

This scenario can be a conversation starter for a number of issues: trust, collaboration, transparency, transformational leadership, and institutional culture to name a few.

Let's start with a meteorological metaphor.[58] Christmas season of 2015 saw unseasonably warm temperatures in many areas of the United States. In the Northeast, for example, traditional ugly holiday sweaters gave way to shorts and T-shirts. Can we conclude that due to this recent temperature change that the culture of that part of the nation will change? Will people decide to toss out their boots and parkas and forever replace them with flip-flops and tank tops? Doubtful. The momentary (climatologically speaking) change will not have a sustainable impact on the behaviors and expectations that have accumulated over the years.

The same in an organization. A new leader (like the dean in the scenario above) can come in and offer a vision of cultural change. But if the leader cannot deliver, then she or he will not affect cultural change. If, for example, a new university president arrives promising sweeping changes (touted for the better in his or her perception), but two, three, or more years later the culture remains, one has to ask, "Why?" Perhaps the new management only provided superficial climate changes.

Or perhaps the administration presents something along the lines of "We will right-size our workforce to better serve our students. We will be more nimble and responsive." In addition to "reorganization," management may bring in new people with identified "skillsets." The spoken word implies a cultural change to provide more appropriate service delivery. Changing the workforce, however, will not in and of itself bring cultural change. In fact, if the new people (part of the climate change) do not fit with the existing culture, damage may be done to what *had been working* in the culture. What the people of the organization may only see is massive job loss and/or salary reductions as well as the hiring of new people who do not appreciate what had been done to build the organization to that point.

Dean Fitzgerald and Associate Dean Wiscot in our scenario above find themselves in the midst of a climate change—and they are finding it will take a lot longer to affect a cultural change at their institution. The dean seems to understand that what remains after his first eighteen months on the job is a lack of trust. For whatever reasons, "buy-in" from faculty still appears a distant dream for cultural shift.

You probably have heard the cliché of "silos" in higher education. A silo by definition is a place to store and protect something such as grain or missiles. On the university or college campus, we are not protecting foodstuffs or armaments, but we can find ourselves protecting positions and turf. Hence we can end up with separate silos for administration, faculty, student affairs, staff, facility custodians, and the like.

Trust is built over time with shared, meaningful, and authentic experiences. It requires a degree of reciprocity in word and deed.

Does your campus seem to lean more toward silos or bridges to collegiality?

• • •

What have we done to make it easier for faculty to understand the administrative perspective?

• • •

Applying The Seven Rs

Before you move on to the next scenario, revisit the seven Rs. What connection(s) can you make between the material presented in this scenario and each of the seven Rs? Once you have completed that, star the

principle (the one "R") that seems to be the most significant in this context and reflect on why you believe this is the most significant principle.

* Relationships
* Relevance
* Rainbows
* Resources
* Responsibility
* Reflection
* Resilience

SCENARIO 30

Syllabus Expectations
and Disconnections

• • •

Organizing Question: How does the classroom instructor create an authentic and healthy relationship in the teaching and learning environment?

Go to www.stevepiscitelli.com for supporting video.

"Professor Kasinski, thank you for taking time today to speak with me. I know you are jammed with midterm exams and the General Education Review Committee work." Dean Roxie motioned to a seat at a small table in the office. She closed the door and sat at the table.

"Is everything OK, dean? I thought our formal evaluation wasn't until the end of the semester?" Professor Kasinski's contract was at this very time making its way through the continuing (tenure) contract committee. She felt a bit vulnerable sitting in the dean's office.

"Oh, fine. Fine. Would you like a bottle of water?" Roxie said as she extended a bottle. The professor accepted the bottle, unscrewed the cap, and took a sip.

"I love what you're doing with the young nursing students," the dean continued. "Your background as a staff nurse for twenty-five years has been absolutely invaluable to our program. I believe our college scored a major coup when you agreed to serve on our nursing faculty. I thoroughly enjoyed my class visit last week. I just wanted to use this time to suggest a little fine-tuning."

Professor Kasinski quickly reviewed the class session the dean referred to in her mind's eye. Nothing particular seemed to immediately stand out that needed "fine-tuning."

"Was there something wrong with what I taught, or was it the way I taught it?"

"Oh heavens, you have the content nailed! No issues there. I noticed, though, a disconnect between the policies in your syllabus and what I observed while sitting in your class. I understand I am just seeing one class session, so maybe it was an aberration. Though, when I think back to last month when I stopped in your class, I observed the same thing."

Professor Kasinski had absolutely no clue what the dean was referencing.

"Your syllabus is a model document. It has personality, it provides clear and high expectations, and it is tightly written. That is so important for our students. They need information in a succinct and accessible manner. Thank you for that."

The professor nodded and smiled at that compliment. Took another sip of water. And waited for the "BUT" that she knew was soon to follow.

"But, again, there were some disconnects that I noticed in the first fifteen minutes I was in the classroom." Roxie opened up her tablet and referenced her notes.

"Although you neatly and clearly spell out the campus policies about drinks being forbidden in the classrooms, I saw at least five students carrying coffee, water, and sodas to their seats. You acknowledged the students but said nothing about the drinks.

"You also state on page three of the syllabus that students need to have their textbooks with them for classwork. When you started your group activity—which I absolutely loved, by the way—there was at least one student in each group without a textbook. Again, you did not say anything.

"And the final—and maybe the biggest disconnect for me and your syllabus expectations—there were at least three students who were constantly tapping on their phones—texting I assume. You said nothing even though you have strict prohibition about such activity during class time. I know I could be missing something. That is why I wanted to speak with you."

Professor Kasinski looked a bit chagrined. "You are correct on all counts, Dean Roxie. No argument from me. I put a lot of strong wording in my syllabus. But when push comes to shove, I know that my students have a lot on their plates. I don't want to become a syllabus monitor. I don't want those policies to get in the way of their getting excited about the content and coming to class. I fear if I become heavy-handed that they will not like me—and I will lose them."

REFLECT ON THIS

* Let's first address the elephant in the corner. What do you think about Professor Kasinski's concern about the students not liking her? Should it ever be a consideration within the teaching and learning environment?
* What about the disconnections between the syllabus and the professor's actions and inactions that the dean noted? Should the professor follow through on her policies and enforce them as stated in the syllabus? If not, should she remove them from the syllabus?
* What policies do you address in your syllabus? Are they nonnegotiable? That is, will you make sure that students adhere to them no questions asked and no exceptions made?
* How do you think the dean handled this situation? Would you have done anything differently if you were the dean?

As you consider the specific reflection questions above, you may wish to give broader thought to the following:

* What VISION do you have concerning expectations in your syllabus for establishing rigor and relationships in the classroom?

* What specific CHALLENGES exist regarding this topic?
* What ACTION will you take to address the challenges and move toward your vision?
* What RESOURCES will you need?

CONSIDER THIS

The syllabus will be one of the most important documents that a student receives in your class. It puts forth expectations and responsibilities for both the students and the instructor. Some schools have mandated templates with required information; others allow for faculty to create their own format while still including required information. This scenario goes beyond what to put in a syllabus. It helps us examine what the faculty member needs to do with the expectations after she clearly states them in the syllabus.

First, let's assume that every expectation and guideline you have listed in your syllabus is appropriate and important enough to be in your document. If your experience resembles mine over my years in the classroom, students do not gleefully jump into reading the syllabus. Some give it a cursory look. Others might flip to the assignment calendar. A few will lose it (assuming you distribute a printed copy in class) before the second class meeting. I distributed a printed copy and posted an online link to the syllabus.

Consider giving a short syllabus quiz either in the first or second week of the session.[59] Mine usually had ten questions. Some semesters the quiz appeared online in the Learning Management System. At times I gave the quiz in class. A few semesters I let the students use their copy of the syllabus during the quiz. Other times I allowed them to collaborate with a classmate. For me the main point was to encourage them to put their eyes on the critical expectations for the semester. This quiz was never (for me) about the grade (which always remained as a minimal part of their overall grade).

For the first three weeks (of a sixteen-week semester), I started each class with a quick review of an important point or two in the syllabus. This modeled the importance of regularly checking the syllabus, and it allowed me, in a reassuring and mindful manner, to reinforce expectations.

Do you take time at the end of the semester to reflect on your syllabus? Not just adjust the dates for the coming term. Rather, do you evaluate the syllabus as a teaching and learning document?

For this reflective exercise,[60] have a copy of your most recent syllabus in front of you. A typical review could include a look at your pacing (did you stay on target?) and your assignments and assessments (did they do what you had thought they would?). Flip through the pages of your syllabus. Pause and observe the structure, the emphases, the length, recurring themes, the detail, and the appearance. Answer the following questions:

* What theme(s) resonated throughout your syllabus?
* What does your syllabus say about you as a teacher?
* If this is the only thing with which a student had to form an opinion about you, what do you think that opinion would be? Does this even matter?
* How do you know your syllabus is effective?
* How could it be more effective? How do you know this is true?
* What will you definitely keep for the next time around—and what will you consider revising or eliminating?
* Did you respect the expectations you placed in the syllabus? Are all of the expectations still pertinent? Do you need to add or delete any?

• • •

***Do you ever take time at the end of the semester
to reflect on your syllabus?***

• • •

APPLYING THE SEVEN RS

Before you move on to the next scenario, revisit the seven Rs. What connection(s) can you make between the material presented in this scenario and each of the seven Rs? Once you have completed that, star the principle (the one "R") that seems to be the most significant in this context and reflect on why you believe this is the most significant principle.

* Relationships
* Relevance
* Rainbows
* Resources
* Responsibility
* Reflection
* Resilience

SCENARIO 31

Your Most Meaningful
Career Accomplishment

• • •

Organizing Question: What single project or task would you consider your most meaningful accomplishment in your career to date?

Go to www.stevepiscitelli.com for supporting video.

IT'S YOUR TURN TO WRITE a scenario.[61] This one focuses on you. Specifically, you have the luxury to reflect on one accomplishment in your career that stands out as the most meaningful for you—whether it was last week or forty years ago. What stands out as your most meaningful accomplishment? Write the answer below or in your personal journal.

1. My most meaningful accomplishment to date: _____
   _____
   _____
   _____
   _____
   _____

Once you have that, now consider the *why* of that *what*. That is, why does this particular accomplishment stand out for you? This can include people you worked with, lessons learned, mistakes made, enthusiasm stoked, and friendships forged. Write your responses below.

2. The reason(s) this accomplishment stands out: _____

_____

_____

_____

_____

_____

Consider the following Venn Diagram as it relates to your meaningful accomplishment. Reflect on the actions you took, the passion you had for the project or task, and the connection to your core values. Were all three engaged by the accomplishment you noted above? (Probably so if, in fact, it has been your most meaningful accomplishment to date.)

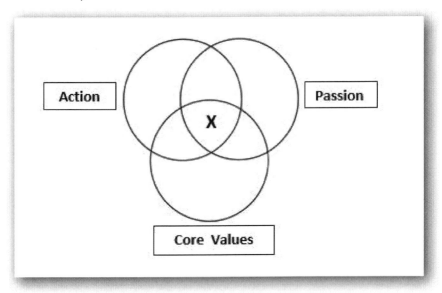

Did your accomplishment hit the sweet spot ("X" marks the sweet spot) for you?

REFLECT ON THIS

* As you consider and decide upon your most meaningful accomplishment, it may take you a while to settle on just one. That's OK. As you do your initial brainstorming, you may wish to keep a list and then return to the other items at a later time.
* Consider some deeper questions such as
    * How do your actions become magnified (and meaningful) when they connect to your passion and core values?
    * When you look at your time in this calling, how often can you say you have hit the sweet spot? You can refer back to your brainstorming list above.
    * What can you do (or, what do you still do) to bring more moments, projects, and tasks like the one you identified above into your day-to-day activities?

As you consider the specific reflection questions above, you may wish to give broader thought to the following:

* What VISION do you have about meaning and passion as they relate to your calling?
* What specific CHALLENGES exist regarding this topic?
* What ACTION will you take to address the challenges and move toward your vision?
* What RESOURCES will you need?

CONSIDER THIS

Here is the path I traveled to settle on my most meaningful accomplishment:

When I did this activity, I thought, "Well, that's easy to answer." And then, I had no answer. I was stumped. I kept coming back to it over the next few days. Was it my first publishing contract? Getting hired by the college?

Speaking engagements around the nation? Establishing a blog? Building a YouTube channel? Mentoring students? A cocurricular activity?

All of those represented powerful steps in my calling, but did they qualify as the "most meaningful accomplishment"?

Finally, as I replayed my teaching years, it hit me. The year was 1983. April 19, 1983, to be exact.

I was in my second year of teaching—and I was teaching seventh-grade geography students. I developed, organized, and orchestrated a Model United Nations for approximately 300 seventh graders.

The students represented nations from around the world. They developed the topic for debate. They researched and role-played "their" nations. We had an international luncheon. Parents were on hand. We developed "Delegate Rules" and learned how to prepare a resolution. The students sent letters (yep, with real postage stamps) to embassies requesting information.

The students learned about public speaking, creative problem solving, diversity, research skills, peer interaction, governments, and political philosophies.

Why was this my most meaningful accomplishment out of all the projects and task in three-plus decades of classroom teaching?

This event hooked me on interactive teaching and learning. It taught me the importance of having supportive supervisors as they let me run with my idea with no micromanaging. They trusted me—a relatively new teacher—to do what was right for my students. I saw upfront and personally the importance of detailed planning and collaboration.

And I learned that no matter how beneficial educational outcomes might be, there would always be those questioning teaching motives. I actually was contacted by a then-state legislator wanting to know what the hidden agenda was with my activity! He had read a report that claimed activities like the Model UN to be questionable, unbalanced, and biased. I assured him my only hidden agenda was how to keep 300 seventh graders on-task for an entire day! And his questioning reminded me to always examine my motivations through various lenses and from differing frames of reference.

That one activity helped me, early on in my calling, to mature as a teacher and classroom leader. I did not receive any special funding; nor did I receive any unique recognition. I did come to understand, though, the importance of psychic wages—the internal reward we get when our actions align with our passion and purpose. For more than thirty years, I continued to follow my instincts and experiential evidence when developing engaging activities for my students (and audiences for professional development events). My actions become magnified (and meaningful) when they connect to my passion and enthusiasm.

My guess is, the same holds true for you.

• • •

That one activity helped me, early on in my calling, to mature as a teacher and classroom leader.

• • •

Applying The Seven Rs

Before you move on to the next scenario, revisit the seven Rs. What connection(s) can you make between the material presented in this scenario and each of the seven Rs? Once you have completed that, star the principle (the one "R") that seems to be the most significant in this context and reflect on why you believe this is the most significant principle.

* Relationships
* Relevance
* Rainbows
* Resources
* Responsibility
* Reflection
* Resilience

SCENARIO 32

Connecting with the Dean

• • •

Organizing Question: In what ways can regularly scheduled and informal meetings with your supervisor deepen collegial connections?

Go to www.stevepiscitelli.com for supporting video.

DEAN SHACKELFORD HAS BEEN IN his current position for three months. He conducts weekly coffee meetings for the faculty he supervises. He told his faculty when he announced the coffee initiative, "These sessions remain voluntary in that they will not be counted 'against you' if you don't come. It remains your choice to come or not come. I believe these sessions will help create a cohesiveness that will allow our department to continue to grow for our students' benefit and also help you and me deepen our collegial connection. Please use this opportunity to speak about whatever you want to with me. I do ask that when you make your appointment that you give me a brief idea about the topic or topics you would like to discuss."

He reserves one ninety-minute block of time each week on the calendar for these chats. Each meeting time (with one faculty member) will be for up to fifteen minutes (it can be less). Follow-up meetings can be scheduled if the faculty member would like. While appointments are not necessary, the dean does suggest them to assure that time will be available when a faculty member stops by.

You like the idea of the dean having this time available. However, earlier today you heard two veteran faculty raising concerns. Based on their past dealings with former deans, your colleagues were concerned that these meetings might be used nefariously to "get something on faculty." There appears to be a trust issue that you were not aware of before. One colleague snidely muttered, "Yeah, voluntary my foot. The dean will mentally ding any faculty member who does not take advantage of this cute ploy."

REFLECT ON THIS

* Would you take advantage of these open-door chats if your dean offered them? Why or why not?
* If you were to attend one of these conversations today, what would be your number one agenda item to discuss?
* Can you think of any reasons why faculty colleagues might be reticent to take advantage of this opportunity?
* Do you believe fifteen minutes can deepen collegial connections?
* If you did have one of these chats with your dean, what would you expect as a result of the time spent?
* What about the colleagues who believe these meetings could be a ploy to hurt or undermine faculty? What can you do with this information?

As you consider the specific reflection questions above, you may wish to give broader thought to the following:

* What VISION do you have when it comes to establishing a meaningful and respectful relationship with your supervisor?
* What specific CHALLENGES exist regarding this topic?
* What ACTION will you take to address the challenges and move toward your vision?
* What RESOURCES will you need?

Consider This

Meetings can be a chore and a bore. Perhaps the last thing you need is to add a one-on-one with your dean to your list of things to do. This scenario, however, does offer a different approach to meetings. Innovative companies have created ways to escape the old meeting paradigm.[62] Perhaps the dean in this scenario might be interested in doing the same.

Consider, though, the opportunity in the scenario above as more of a conversation than a meeting. It becomes a time for two professionals to sit down and have a discussion about matters of importance.

One challenge in this case might well rest with the *limited* amount of time. Since, at most, the dean could have six fifteen-minute meetings in one block of time, he and the faculty member will need to be prepared and efficient with the brief time. The benefit comes from the open line of communication that is being developed (or, maybe maintained) in your workplace. The intent can be powerful. The execution may need fine-tuning.

The dean understands that collegiality comes down to three things: Relationships. Relationships. Relationships.

• • •

Underscore the importance of developing voluntary and open lines of communication (as opposed to chain-of-command enforced meetings).

• • •

Applying The Seven Rs

Before you move on to the next scenario, revisit the seven Rs. What connection(s) can you make between the material presented in this scenario and each of the seven Rs? Once you have completed that, star the

principle (the one "R") that seems to be the most significant in this context and reflect on why you believe this is the most significant principle.

- Relationships
- Relevance
- Rainbows
- Resources
- Responsibility
- Reflection
- Resilience

Know When to Say "No!"

• • •

***Organizing Question: Is there an appropriate time and an effective way
to say "No"?***

Go to www.stevepiscitelli.com for supporting video.

MARTHA COMPLETED HER FIRST YEAR of teaching—and she did it well.
Her supervisor evaluated her as "Excellent" in the categories of classroom
management, professional development, committee work, cocurricular
involvement, and overall collegiality. She did note one area of concern
in the annual evaluation. And that was in the area of "Balance and Well-
being." While this was not an "official" category on the evaluation, Dean
Getsit took time to write a narrative on the final page of the evaluation
instrument. Today she is meeting with her faculty colleague to discuss the
evaluation and improvement plan.

"Martha, you have proven to be a wonderful asset to our campus and
our students. You have done more in your first year than most faculty do
in their first five years."

Martha beamed with satisfaction. "Thank you, dean. That means a
great deal coming from you. I have attempted to be as involved as I can in
the campus life and governance. I have had some wonderful role models."

The dean continued. "Interesting that you mention that, because I do
have one major concern: Your health and well-being. While I applaud your
willingness to be involved, I fear you may be stretching yourself a bit thin. I
don't want you to burn out before your time. At times it is OK to say 'No.'"

Martha chuckled. "I've been told that by those closest to me all my life. I'll have plenty of time to slow down later in my career. Right now, there is so much I want to learn. And, truth be told, I want to build a name for myself at this institution. I'm not one to fly under the radar. And if someone asks me to be involved, my default is always to say 'Yes!' I want to be known as a team player who has a lot to offer. I guess I adhere to the philosophy from a Neil Young lyric, 'It's better to burn out than fade away.' I'll be fine. But thanks for the concern."

From over the top of her glasses, the dean looked at her newest faculty member, not sure where to go next with the conversation. "You know," she thought to herself, "there's another line in that song that she may want to consider, 'Once you're gone, you can't come back.'"§§§

Reflect on This

* If you sat in Dean Getsit's chair, would you broach this situation with Martha? Why or why not?
* How do you believe the dean should respond to Martha's "It's better to burn out than fade away"?
* Is it better to say "No" than "Yes"? If it is better, then where does one draw that line?
* Should new faculty members be concerned about "building a name" for themselves?
* What role should the department chair and dean play with new faculty in situations such as presented in the scenario? Should the chair act as a mentor for balance and well-being?

As you consider the specific reflection questions above, you may wish to give broader thought to the following:

---

§§§ To hear or view Neil Young's lyrics for this song, type "My My, Hey Hey (Into the Black)" into your favorite search engine."

* What VISION do you have regarding your boundaries, limits, and well-being?
* What specific CHALLENGES exist regarding this topic?
* What ACTION will you take to address the challenges and move toward your vision?
* What RESOURCES will you need?

CONSIDER THIS

On the positive side, the professor in our scenario (Martha) remains motivated and full of energy. The dean sees her as a real asset to the faculty ranks. The dean, also, can represent another bright spot in this scenario. She is a supervisor asking her faculty colleague to consider pulling back and making sure she takes care of herself. She appears to understand the importance of life balance.

One study, found that 82 percent of higher faculty felt stressed or burned out due to lack of personal time.[63] Nearly 85 percent of the same undergraduate faculty population admitted that their own self-imposed high expectations created stress in their lives.

What can you do so as not to become a burnout statistic (see Scenario 6)?

One thing that may help is whether or not you have established set, articulated, and understood boundaries and limits. A *boundary* is what you set for other people—that line in the sand that you ask them not to cross. A *limit*, on the other hand, represents what you set for yourself—the line that you wish not to cross. (See Scenario 14.)

Consider what you do to maintain balance in your life on and off the job. What do you do to maintain well-being and balance? How do you integrate life, family, and personal expectations? How do you stay resilient?

• • •

What can you do so as not to become a burnout statistic?

• • •

APPLYING THE SEVEN Rs

Before you move on to the next scenario, revisit the seven Rs. What connection(s) can you make between the material presented in this scenario and each of the seven Rs? Once you have completed that, star the principle (the one "R") that seems to be the most significant in this context and reflect on why you believe this is the most significant principle.

* Relationships
* Relevance
* Rainbows
* Resources
* Responsibility
* Reflection
* Resilience

Let Me Show You How It's Done

• • •

Organizing Question: What is the most effective strategy for mentoring a colleague about classroom management skills?

Go to www.stevepiscitelli.com for supporting video.

PROFESSOR TOOTLE IS A SECOND-YEAR faculty member at City Community College. She teaches, among other preparations, a writing class. While she has command of the material, she feels like she is floundering when it comes to getting her students actively engaged in class discussions. The semester has been underway for four weeks, and she does not know what else to do to get the students more interested and involved in class discussions. She asked her colleague, Professor Ledge, to observe one class session. Professor Ledge has been teaching at CCC for twenty-two years.

On the agreed-upon day, as students entered class, Professor Ledge found a seat in the back of the room. Professor Tootle acknowledged her colleague's entrance with a smile and a wave from the front of the room where she was preparing for the day's lesson. At the top of the hour, Tootle commenced the lesson.

"Class, today we are going to talk about the concept of integrity in journalism." She walked to the board and wrote the word. "First, for the next five minutes, I want you to write in your notes what the term 'integrity' means to you." With that, Tootle returned to her desk, sat down, and worked at the computer.

Professor Ledge looked around the room and saw the following:

* In every row of the classroom, at least one student appeared to be texting.
* The student sitting next to her typed furiously on her tablet. Unfortunately, she was typing an update on a social-media site.
* One student in the back of the room was sleeping.
* Another student's cell phone rang. The student answered it as she exited the classroom.
* Five students entered the room late.
* Two students were whispering to each other.
* One student looked to be doing math homework.
* A handful of students were writing something in their notebooks.

Five minutes elapsed, and Professor Tootle stood up from her desk and walked to the center of the room. "OK! Who would like to share their thoughts about integrity?"

Nothing. Not one student spoke up.

"Tom," Tootle motioned to a boy in the back of the room, "what did you come up with?"

Tom shrugged his shoulders. "I'm still thinking."

Professor Ledge was getting antsy watching this unfold. "This is killing me," she thought. "Why doesn't she connect the assignment to something specific in the course material to get them started?"

A few more futile minutes went by. The students did not engage the conversation. Finally, Ledge raised her hand to catch the attention of her colleague. "May I say something?" And with that the veteran professor stood up and walked to the front of the room before her colleague could respond.

"Hi, I'm Professor Ledge," she said with a smile. "Professor Tootle has given you a great opportunity to reflect on a relevant question. You seem to be having difficulty with this. Oh, you there," she pointed to a texting student in the back of the room. "Put that away now, please."

"Now, let's connect this concept of integrity to your assignment for the day. Open your books." With that Professor Ledge took control of the lesson. Professor Tootle took a seat at her computer desk and watched.

REFLECT ON THIS

- Evaluate Professor Tootle's opening and directions to her class. What worked? What did not work? How would you have orchestrated this beginning?
- Can you think of a more effective way for Professor Tootle to have introduced the topic of integrity to the class?
- Refer to the student behaviors (above list) that Professor Ledge observed while she sat in the back of the room. What can you infer from the level of student engagement that is taking place?
- How would you classify the student behaviors? Class management? Content management? Civility? Something else?
- Evaluate Professor Ledge's behavior when she stepped to the front of the class? Appropriate? Impact on Professor Tootle? Message to the students? How would you feel if you were Tootle? How would you have handled the situation if you were Professor Ledge?

As you consider the specific reflection questions above, you may wish to give broader thought to the following:

- What VISION do you have regarding collegial feedback and mentoring?
- What specific CHALLENGES exist regarding this topic?
- What ACTION will you take to address the challenges and move toward your vision?
- What RESOURCES will you need?

Consider This

Whether formal or informal, a mentoring program benefits the mentee, the mentor, the students, and the institution. Remember, though, that we need *effective* mentoring. Just the act of observing and giving feedback does not necessarily make one a mentor. In our scenario above, Professor Ledge appears to be acting in an informal capacity with Professor Tootle. So far, great. Such a relationship can validate and build a collaborative spirit for both professors. The fact that Tootle felt comfortable and secure enough to seek out her more experienced colleague speaks volumes for the new faculty's awareness of her own vulnerabilities. She appears willing to learn.

While some might see a difference,[64] effective *mentors* understand that they do act as *coaches* for their mentees. And while different coaches have their own personalities and approaches, it is important to understand that the basic building block has to be a respectful relationship between the two.

Was Professor Ledge respectful toward her colleague? Did she "show up" Professor Tootle? Was she merely impatient? Did she miss an important teaching and learning moment for her momentary mentee?

Consider different ways the situation could have been handled. A few thoughts include:

* Professor Ledge could have quietly moved to the front of the room and spoke with her colleague during the time the students were supposed to be working on the assignment.
* Professor Ledge could have made note of all the behaviors that she saw and then discussed them with Tootle after class.
* Professor Ledge could invite Professor Tootle to her classroom to observe a lesson. At that time, Ledge could model how she would handle a similar class assignment.

There remains one other consideration that at times might be lost in a mentoring relationship. The veteran teacher does not always have the answers or the best ways to engage a class. Sometimes new teachers might prove to be great mentors themselves. Sometimes the mentee might be able to mentor the mentor about new strategies or new content or improved strategies.

There is no need to be an island.

• • •

We need effective mentoring.

• • •

Applying The Seven Rs

Before you move on to the next scenario, revisit the seven Rs. What connection(s) can you make between the material presented in this scenario and each of the seven Rs? Once you have completed that, star the principle (the one "R") that seems to be the most significant in this context and reflect on why you believe this is the most significant principle.

- Relationships
- Relevance
- Rainbows
- Resources
- Responsibility
- Reflection
- Resilience

OMG, Indeed!

• • •

Organizing Question: How will you help students develop more effective communication skills?

Go to www.stevepiscitelli.com for supporting video.

"What on earth is this?" Professor Incredulous muttered to himself as he looked at his tablet prior to the start of the faculty meeting. "Totally disrespectful and uncalled for. Shear laziness. Really?"

"Problem?" asked a colleague, who was thumbing through the agenda and sitting to his right.

"Problem? Yeah, there's a problem! These students have no clue how to type an email. From their nonexistent grammar to their expectation of an immediate response, they show a consistent lack of understanding of where they are—and who we are. Every other line has a *pleeeeeeeeeease* or a *NOW* or a *heeeeelllllpppp*." Professor Incredulous was working himself into a frenzied state.

"Well, it's just an email," replied the other professor somewhat nonplussed. "And, I don't think they mean any harm as much as they are just oblivious to what is proper email netiquette. You know, they're so used to text messaging and abbreviations. It's a whole new world out there, my friend. To our students, email is *so yesterday.*"

Thrusting his tablet in front of his colleague's face, Incredulous couldn't contain his distain. "Look at this drivel. No harm, you say! I get student essays that look like this; phone messages that aren't much better.

There is a pervasive disregard for the English language, civility, and respect for us! How are they going to make it in the workforce with this kind of communication? Or I should say *lack* of communication." He pulled the tablet back in front of himself and began typing furiously.

"I'll just give this self-entitled millennial a taste of his own medicine. See how he likes getting a grammatically incorrect and incoherent email! And for good measure, I think I will demand his immediate response by reporting to my office before he enters class tomorrow. And for good measure, I'll type in ALL CAPS! OMG, indeed!"

REFLECT ON THIS

+ Have you had a similar experience with student communication to the one Professor Incredulous describes? How did you handle it?
+ Respond to the colleague who said, "It's just an email...They are just oblivious...." Do you agree or disagree?
+ What do you think about Professor Incredulous's reaction and his decision to give the student "a taste of his own medicine"?
+ Should the professor just ignore the student's email errors and consider it a sign of the changing times? Again, as his colleague said, is "email is *so yesterday*"?

As you consider the specific reflection questions above, you may wish to give broader thought to the following:

+ What VISION do you have regarding professional, civil, and appropriate student communication?
+ What specific CHALLENGES exist regarding communication with students?
+ What ACTION will you take to address the challenges and move toward your vision?
+ What RESOURCES will you need?

CONSIDER THIS

Let's start with a question, "What is the elephant in the room?" Ostensibly, this scenario concerns itself with what one professor considers to be an inappropriately written student email. On further examination, a number of issues present themselves for consideration and discussion with your colleagues:

- Professor Incredulous seems put-off by the grammar and informality of the email. While "they should know better" might be one response from professors, the reality might be closer to the colleague in the above scenario. Our students (especially those knowing only a world of social media and 140 character bursts of communication) may not know better when it comes to emails. Consider such incidents as teaching and learning moments.

- Is email "so yesterday"? Is it, in other words, outdated, archaic and not representative of the second decade of the twenty-first century? Should we move to where the students find themselves and communicate with them via social-media platforms and texting? Or perhaps communicating through your school's learning management system (LMS) might prove helpful. We would do well to at least consider that we (as a society) began our love affair with email before we had our cell phones. Email was, at the time, one of the quickest (maybe the quickest?) ways to reach out to someone who was not in front of us at that moment. Cell phones and tablets have changed the dynamics. It might, at the least, be a conversation to consider having (or continue having) in your institution.

- Do the concerns offered in this scenario stop with email or have you and your colleagues seen such issues arise in written assignments and phone messages?

- Since email, in spite of the talk of its demise,[65] still exists in the workplace, are we professionally responsible to teach our students the basics of email etiquette (netiquette)? Should we approach it as a workplace skill?

- Perhaps this would be one of the many areas in which classroom teachers can introduce the students to the boundaries and limits of their classes. Do you clearly state your expected response time to emails and phone calls (in the syllabus for example)? This could be addressed during the first day of class as well.

- When I emailed my students, I did my best to model appropriate netiquette. On occasion, I would share in class an inappropriate email I had received (minus any identifiers about whom wrote the email). I would then ask the students to identify the appropriate and inappropriate sections of the email. For the inappropriate parts, students suggested improvement. Rather than scold and rant (like Professor Incredulous above), this strategy involved my students in the process of teaching and learning.

• • •

Are we professionally responsible to teach our students the basics of email etiquette (netiquette)?

• • •

Applying The Seven Rs

Before you move on to the next scenario, revisit the seven Rs. What connection(s) can you make between the material presented in this scenario and each of the seven Rs? Once you have completed that, star the principle (the one "R") that seems to be the most significant in this context and reflect on why you believe this is the most significant principle.

- Relationships
- Relevance
- Rainbows
- Resources

- Responsibility
- Reflection
- Resilience

Everyone Gets a Trophy!

• • •

Organizing Question: How would you develop a meaningful and effective employee recognition program?

Go to www.stevepiscitelli.com for supporting video.

"GOT A MOMENT?" ASKED PROFESSOR Hadit as he stood at his colleague's office door.

"Sure, come on in, Don. Have a seat." Professor Binder pointed to the seat at the side of his desk. Both professors taught in the English department on their campus. Don Hadit was the current department chair. He had been in that position for two years.

"Not sure where to start, Ann, other than this is the stereotypical case of doing what I thought was right only to catch grief from every direction. Remember the campus meeting we had last week with the campus president?"

"Yeah," replied Ann. "I thought it went well. Very positive. Especially the recognition of the 'all-stars' in each of the departments. Finally, nice to see faculty recognized for what they do well."

"Well, there's the rub," said Don with a sigh. "We, the department chairs, were asked to pass along the names of some of our faculty who have done something well over the last semester. We could only give four or five names. The president wanted to reach out and thank those folks. So,

I did that. Thought it was a good idea, too. Unfortunately, my phone has not stopped ringing, the email inbox keeps dinging, and there have been a few unpleasant conversations—or should I say diatribes—in my office."

"I don't understand," offered a confused-looking Ann. "About positive recognition?"

"Yeah. It seems people got very upset—I mean red-in-the-face mad—that *they* weren't recognized. Some went as far as to tell me why the people I chose were not deserving of such recognition. I'm flabbergasted. Feeling a bit blindsided. Even had one person claim the only reason you were recognized is because we are friends outside of campus. Geez. Since I observe every teacher in this department and conduct thorough evaluations, I thought I was in the best place to be objective."

Ann raised her eyebrows and blew a slow breath.

"I'm not sure how to rebound from this one. Frankly, I'm mad as hell. Got any thoughts?" asked Professor Hadit as he slumped into the chair and stared straight ahead at the wall. "I feel like we're stuck in a place where everyone has to get a trophy!"

REFLECT ON THIS

- Does this scenario seem farfetched? Would seasoned professionals act in this manner?
- Do you agree with Professor Hadit's observation that "everyone has to get a trophy"?
- If you were in Professor Hadit's position, would you have proceeded any differently when asked by the campus president for a few of the "all-stars" in your department? Briefly explain.
- How does your department and institution recognize its all-stars?

As you consider the specific reflection questions above, you may wish to give broader thought to the following:

- What VISION do you have for recognizing outstanding colleagues for their efforts on behalf of students and colleagues?
- What specific CHALLENGES exist with employee recognition?
- What ACTION will you take to address the challenges and move toward your vision?
- What RESOURCES will you need?

CONSIDER THIS

Recognizing faculty for a "job well done" seems like commonsense to overall faculty development. But while the intention may seem admirable, the execution might prove more difficult. Many institutions honor faculty with outstanding faculty awards. Some national organizations do the same.[66] This scenario does not address anything so formal. It appears to have been an attempt by the campus president to reach out and say "thank you." The department chairs cooperated. And then all hell seems to have broken loose.

I have run into this type of scenario in my career. Is the elephant in the room known as "favoritism" or "peevishness" or something else? Or maybe, just maybe, the complaining faculty do have a gripe about who was singled out and who was not.

As you and your colleagues grapple with this scenario, maybe one place to start is by considering if Professor Hadit works in an environment where everyone believes he or she is excellent. If that is the case, then hasn't "excellent" in that environment actually become "average"? Excellent indicates far above the average.

What represents average teaching and what looks like excellent teaching at your institution?

• • •

When it comes to faculty recognition, while the intention may seem admirable, the execution might prove more difficult.

• • •

Applying The Seven Rs

Before you move on to the next scenario, revisit the seven Rs. What connection(s) can you make between the material presented in this scenario and each of the seven Rs? Once you have completed that, star the principle (the one "R") that seems to be the most significant in this context and reflect on why you believe this is the most significant principle.

* Relationships
* Relevance
* Rainbows
* Resources
* Responsibility
* Reflection
* Resilience

Now It's Your Turn

• • •

Organizing Question: What particular situation in your campus and institutional culture lends itself to its own scenario to stimulate meaningful collegial conversations?

Go to www.stevepiscitelli.com for supporting video.

YOU HAVE HAD THE OPPORTUNITY to work on more than thirty scenarios in this book. Each one focused on one or more aspects of the teaching and learning process. Hopefully, each scenario helped you to clarify and/ or sharpen your thoughts and practices. Moreover, each scenario provided an opportunity to work with colleagues. May those conversations continue.

Now it's time for you to apply the same scenario process to your campus and institutional culture. What topics, situations, events, or issues present themselves on your campus that have not been addressed in the foregoing scenarios? Perhaps you and some colleagues can start by listing the top five or ten topics for discussion. Then prioritize the list. And then write your own scenario that brings the top issue to life. Your scenario need not be long; a few paragraphs can suffice to get the information across.

Once you have completed the scenario, add three to five items in the "Reflect on This" section. Use the previous scenarios as a guide to get your thought process started.

Then complete your own "Consider This" section. Again, see the previous pages for examples.

You may find that you will come up with a different format for your scenario. Great! Find and use your own voice for this. Own it! Above all, keep the conversation going.

Reflect on This

-
-
-
-
-

As you consider the specific reflection questions above, you may wish to give broader thought to the following:

- What VISION do you have regarding this topic?
- What specific CHALLENGES exist regarding this topic?
- What ACTION will you take to address the challenges and move toward your vision?
- What RESOURCES will you need?

Consider This

-
-
-
-
-

• • •

Identify the main issue you would like to address on your campus.

• • •

APPLYING THE SEVEN RS

Revisit the seven Rs. What connection(s) can you make between the material presented in this scenario and each of the seven Rs? Once you have completed that, star the principle (the one "R") that seems to be the most significant in this context and reflect on why you believe this is the most significant principle.

* Relationships
* Relevance
* Rainbows
* Resources
* Responsibility
* Reflection
* Resilience

APPENDIX A

• • •

THE FOLLOWING LIST OF QUESTIONS provide for a more in-depth examination of Scenario 4 ("The First Day of Class").

Consider this mantra for the first day of class: People Before Paper! In a word: Relationships. Establish a human connection. Below you will find a few suggestions on applying the topics and questions to your campus culture. Do not attempt to answer all questions at one sitting. The intent is not to overwhelm but, rather, to help you clarify. Use the list of questions to stimulate conversations. For instance, you could:

- Choose a particular category that you would like to examine and discuss.
- Match a category to a particular challenge you have—or your faculty colleagues have identified.
- Prioritize the list according to your needs (your colleagues' needs, your students' needs). And then, starting with the biggest priority items, use the list as a weekly lunch-and-learn agenda.
- Distribute the list with a new faculty-orientation packet—and then use the questions during mentor-mentee sessions.
- From the list below, develop your own "Top Ten Questions" every faculty member needs to ask before going into the first day of class.
- For the more theatrical, perform role plays that bring the categories and questions to life.
- Ask your student leaders what they would add to the list.

Here is my suggested list of planning questions:[67]

* Announcements. What announcements do you want to make at the beginning of class? What announcements will you want to make before dismissing the class for the first day? What will your parting (last) words for the day be to your students? How do you want them to remember you and the class?
* Attire. Do you think your attire impacts the impression your students have of you? How do you know? What will you wear? Why?
* Baggage. How will you convey to students that the classroom is their time to explore, be curious, learn—and focus on themselves and their growth? What will you do to encourage them to "check" their personal "baggage" at the door each day? How will you "check" your own "baggage" each day?
* Boundaries and Limits. What boundaries (how far students can go) will you be sure to emphasize the first day? What limits (how far you will go) will you express?
* Civility. What will you do to encourage civility in your classroom? How will you respond to acts of incivility?
* Class from Hell. From students' perspectives and experiences, what makes for a terrible class? What did the professor do? What did the students do?[68]
* Class rules. What are your major rules for the class? Are there any rules for the class? How will you communicate the rules?
* Goal. What is one overriding and one specific goal you have for the first day of class?
* Gratitude. How will you show gratitude to your students? How will you encourage them to show gratitude to the class?
* Heavenly Class. From students' perspectives and experiences, what makes for a great class? What did the professor do? What did the students do?
* Honest Feedback. How will you get honest feedback from your students about the first day in class? Will you ask general questions

in a class discussion, ask for anonymous written responses before they leave class or assume if no one asks questions all is OK?

- Icebreaker/Community Building. What initial activities will you do on this first day to begin the process of building a community for teaching and learning? Do you believe building a classroom community is important? Why or why not?

- Initial Greeting. How will you greet students before the "formal" introductions (see below)? Where and when will you do this?

- Introductions: Them. What will you ask the students to share with the class about themselves? Will you ask them to share anything? Why or why not? How will you guide them and make them feel at ease?

- Introductions: You. How will you introduce yourself? Will you simply be the disembodied "Professor So-and-So"? Will you share something "human" about your life—and your journey to the classroom? If you could only share three appropriate things with your students about who you are, what would those three be? Why did you choose to share these? How self-revelatory will you be? What is appropriate? Inappropriate?

- Names. How will you remember the names of your students? How will you encourage them to know the names of their classmates? Why would you even want to do this? Will you use photographs of students to help you remember names? Do you think it's important to remember names?

- Passion. What will you do to demonstrate your authentic enthusiasm and excitement for the class and course material? How will you show authentic excitement for their (your students') presence?

- Relevance. What will you do to establish relevance between the course and the students' lives? How will you demonstrate this course has meaning to their dreams?

- Resources. Are there any campus, community, or career resources you want your students to be familiar with from the first day of the semester?

- Seating. Will you require students to sit in assigned seats? If they can choose their seats, do they have to sit in the same one all semester? Can they sit in any seat at any time during the term?
- Social Media. Will you use social media for class communication and lessons? Will you accept "friend" requests on social media?
- Syllabus. Do you plan to distribute the syllabus on the first day of class? If you do, will you read it to the class? Why or why not? What will you do with the syllabus once you distribute it to the students?
- Technology and Classroom Preparation. When will you examine the technology available in the classroom? Will you go to the classroom before class begins on day one so that it (the computer or the projector, for example) is up and running when the students arrive—or will you use the first few minutes of class to do that while the students are getting settled? When will you know if the room can accommodate the number of students enrolled in the class? Is this important?
- Timeliness. Will you be in class early, right on time, or whenever the mood hits you? Will you require punctuality from your students? If so, how will you explain this to them? Your reasoning?
- Trust. What will you do on this first day to begin the process of trust building in the classroom? What will you do to begin the process of establishing the classroom as a "safe place" for expressing views and opinions? Do you want the students to express their views and opinions?

GRATITUDE!

• • •

Go to www.stevepiscitelli.com for supporting video.

AUTHORS TYPE THE WORDS AND create the work. They structure the book. Their names go on the cover and book spine. But the final product represents the collaborative product of so many people.

Such is the case with *Stories about Teaching, Learning, and Resilience: No Need to Be an Island.* So many colleagues and friends gave of their valuable time to review various pieces of this work. The quality of the book you have in front is in no small way due to these fine folks. Any shortcomings belong totally to me.

Whether they reviewed a scenario or two, the front matter or end matter, advised me on style, kept my sentences parallel, or identified errant or missing commas, their collective efforts emphasizes the main theme of this book—there is no need to be an island. I have listed the following in alphabetical order (by first names).

*Amy Perkins (Director of Title IX Coordination and former Dean of Student Success, Florida State College at Jacksonville)
*Ann M. Pearson (Paperback Writer)
*Ashli Archer (Professor, Florida State College at Jacksonville)
*Edward J Leach (Executive Director of NISOD, The University of Texas at Austin)

*Eileen Crawford (Licensed Mental Health Counselor)

*Emily Moore (Associate Professor, Wake Technical Community College)

*Frances Villagran-Glover (Dean, Northern Virginia Community College)

*Jackie Freeze, PhD (Administrator Emeritus, Western Wyoming Community College)

*Jill Simons (Assistant Vice Chancellor, Undergraduate Studies Arkansas State University)

*JoAnn Carpenter (Professor, Florida State College)

*John J. "Ski" Sygielski (President, HACC, Central Pennsylvania's Community College)

*Karen Armstrong (Career Counselor, Penn State University)

*Keri Dutkiewicz (Director of Faculty Learning, Davenport University)

*Lori Dees (Associate Professor, Wake Technical Community College)

*Mary Boone Treuting (Professor of Psychology and Director of the Centers for Academic Success and Teaching Excellence, Louisiana State University of Alexandria)

*Miriam Folk (Professor, Florida State College at Jacksonville)

*Patrick D. McDermott (Associate Professor, College Success & Career Planning, Tallahassee Community College)

*Rex J. Cogdill (Vice President for Student Services, Eastern Wyoming College)

*Sheri Brown (Reference Librarian, Florida State College at Jacksonville)

*Terry O'Banion (Chair of the Graduate Faculty, National American University)

*Todd A. Stanislav (Director, Faculty Center for Teaching and Learning, Ferris State University)

I also want to thank:

*My Amazon CreateSpace consultant, Jenny Chandler, for helping me initially navigate the publishing piece of this work. And all of the consultants who took time to help me understand and work through the publishing process.

*The innovators of Innovative Educators (www.innovativeeducators.org) for providing critical feedback on the videos that accompany this book.

*My wonderful wife, Laurie, for her patience during this process. She was never too busy to listen and to offer suggestions when I was stuck or feeling overwhelmed. I'm glad she's on the island with me.

*Roxie, my canine companion, for walking me to the beach each morning to start our day with a calming sunrise before I hunkered down at the computer. She listened to me sort things out.

And I am grateful for where I live—Atlantic Beach, Florida. While it is truly a geographic island, I never feel alone, as it remains my go-to-place to foster my resilience.

Steve Piscitelli
Atlantic Beach, FL
2017

ABOUT THE AUTHOR

• • •

STEVE PISCITELLI DRAWS ON MORE than three decades of teaching experience. A retired professor, he continues to work as an interactive training facilitator and keynote speaker. His experiences have introduced him to the many challenges educators face nationwide. Piscitelli shares his resources for growth and resilience with his blog, podcast, and videos.

Piscitelli has authored books and articles on student success principles and strategies. In 2014, Piscitelli delivered a TEDx talk entitled "Awareness, Assumptions, and Actions: Why Do You Do What You Do?"

His recognitions include receiving his college's Outstanding Faculty Award, serving as his college's chair for the Center of Teaching and Learning, being named as one of the "Fabulous 50" at Florida State College at Jacksonville, and being listed by his alma mater, Jacksonville University, as one of the "Alumni You Ought to Know."

Piscitelli lives with his wife, Laurie, and canine companion, Roxie, in Atlantic Beach, Florida.

You can learn more about Steve and his resources at www.stevepiscitelli.com.

WORKS CITED

• • •

Andersen, Travis. "Harvard Professor Says Grade Inflation Rampant." BostonGlobe.com. December 4, 2013.

Berger, Warren. *A More Beautiful Question: The Power of Inquiry to Spark Breakthrough Ideas.* New York: Bloomsbury, 2014.

Blanda, Sean. "How to Run Your Meetings like Apple and Google." *Behance: Empowering the Creative Community.*

Brookfield, Stephen D. *Becoming a Critically Reflective Teacher.* San Francisco, CA: John Wiley and Sons, 1995.

Brown, Brené. *Daring Greatly: How the Courage to be Vulnerable Transforms the Way We Live Love, Parent, and Lead.* New York: Gotham Books, 2012.

Burgman, Raymonda, "Avoiding Queen Bee Syndrome." *Inside Higher Ed.* April 20, 2016. https://www.insidehighered.com/advice/2016/04/20/how-deal-conflict-mentorship-experience-essay.

Calhoun Community College. Accessed August 15, 2016. www.calhoun.edu.

Carpenter, Rusty. "An Innovative Plan for Assessing Faculty Development." New Forums. Last modified May 4, 2016. http://newforums.com/an-innovative-plan-for-assessing-faculty-development/.

Carr, Nicholas. *The Shallows: What the Internet is Doing to Our Brains.* New York: W. W. Norton, 2011.

Chickering, A. W., and Z. F. Gamson. "Seven Principles of Good Practice in Undergraduate Education." *American Association for Higher Education* Fall (1987): 2–6.

The College Board. "Quick Guide: College Costs." *Big Future.* https://bigfuture.collegeboard.org/pay-for-college/college-costs/quick-guide-college-costs.

Coyle, Daniel. *The Little Book of Talent.* New York: Bantam Books, 2012.

Cuseo, Joe, Viki S. Fecas, and Aaron Thompson. *Thriving in College & Beyond: Research-Based Strategies for Academic Success & Personal Development.* Dubuque, IA: Kendall/Hunt. 2016.

Cuseo, Joe. "The 'Big Picture': Key Causes of Student Attrition & Key Components of a Comprehensive Student Retention Plan." December 2010. https://www.researchgate.net/publication/237318088_The_BIG_PICTURE_Key_Causes_of_Student_Attrition_Key_Components_of_a_Comprehensive_Student_Retention_Plan.

DeAngelis, Tori. "Unmasking 'Racial' Micro Aggressions." *American Psychological Association* 40, no. 2 (2009).

DePauw University. "Build Team and Trust and You'll Succeed, Duke's 'Coach K' Says in Ubben Lecture." News and Media, September 12, 2002.

Feld, Gordon B. and Susanne Diekelmann. "Sleep Smart: Optimizing Sleep for Declarative Learning and Memory." *Frontiers in Psychology.* May 12, 2015.

File, Thom and Camille Ryan. "Computer and Internet Use in the United States: 2013." American Community Survey Reports. US Census Bureau. November 2014. https://www.census.gov/history/pdf/2013computeruse.pdf.

Flanagan, Caitlin. "That's Not Funny!" *The Atlantic.* September 2015. http://www.theatlantic.com/magazine/archive/2015/09/thats-not-funny/399335/.

Goleman, Daniel. "Empathy 101." October 13, 2013. http://www.daniel-goleman.info/empathy-101/.

Grohol, John M. "FOMO Addiction: The Fear of Missing Out." *World of Psychology* (blog). PsychCentral. April, 14, 2011, http://psychcentral.com/blog/archives/2011/04/14/fomo-addiction-the-fear-of-missing-out/.

Guertin, Laura. "Getting Students to Read the Syllabus with a Syllabus Quiz." *AGU Blogosphere* (blog), August 27, 2014, http://blogs.agu.org/geoedtrek/2014/08/27/syllabus-quiz/.

Hatfield, Susan Rickey. *The Seven Principles in Action: Improving Undergraduate Education.* Bolton, MA: Anker, 1995.

Honolulu Community College. "Faculty Development: Teaching Tips Index," http://www.honolulu.hawaii.edu/facdev/guidebk/teachtip/teachtip.htm, accessed November 10, 2016.

Hsieh, Tony. *Delivering Happiness: A Path to Profits, Passion, and Purpose.* New York: Business Plus, 2010.

Hurtado, Sylvia, et al. "Undergraduate Teaching Faculty: The 2010–2011 HERI Faculty Survey." Higher Education Research Institute at UCLA. Graduate School of Education and Information Studies. University of California, Los Angeles, 2012.

Jaschik, Scott, "Grade Inflation, Higher and Higher. *Inside Higher Ed.* March 29, 2016, https://www.insidehighered.com/news/2016/03/29/survey-finds-grade-inflation-continues-rise-four-year-colleges-not-community-college.

Jiwa, Bernadette. *Meaningful: A Story of Ideas that Fly.* Australia: Perceptive, 2015. Kindle edition.

LaFrance, Adrienne. "The Triumph of Email." *The Atlantic.* January 6, 2016, http://www.theatlantic.com/technology/archive/2016/01/what-comes-after-email/422625/.

Lee, John, *The Anger Solution: The Proven Method for Achieving Calm and Developing Healthy, Long-Lasting Relationships.* Cambridge, MA: Da Capo Press, 2009.

Levine, Arthur and Diane R. Dean. *Generation on a Tightrope: A Portrait of Today's College Student.* San Francisco, CA: John Wiley and Sons, 2012.

Lunde, Joyce Povlacs. "101 Things You Can Do in the First Three Weeks of Class." University of Nebraska-Lincoln. Office of Graduate Studies, http://www.unl.edu/gradstudies/current/teaching/first-3-weeks, accessed November 14, 2016.

Lukianoff, Greg and Jonathan Haidt. "The Coddling of the American Mind." *The Atlantic.* September 2015, http://www.theatlantic.com/magazine/archive/2015/09/the-coddling-of-the-american-mind/399356/.

Medina, John. *Brain Rules: 12 Principles for Surviving and Thriving at Work, Home, and School.* Seattle, WA: Pear, 2008.

National Institute for Staff and Organizational Development (NISOD) and its Excellence Awards, http://nisod.org/?q=products/excellence-awards, accessed November 14, 2016.

National Wellness Institute. "About Wellness," http://www.nationalwellness.org/?page=AboutWellness, accessed November 14, 2016.

Patron, Tim. "From the Court to the Classroom: The 'Fist' Team Analogy," *Duke Master of Management Student Blog.* February 14, 2014.

Piscitelli, Steve. "Are You Relevant?" *The Growth and Resilience Network* (blog). November 8, 2015. https://stevepiscitelli.wordpress.com/2015/11/08/.

———. "Awareness, Assumptions, and Actions. Why Do You Do What You Do?" A TEDx-FSCJ Talk. November 3, 2014. www.youtube.com/watch?v=HZQ2GEhoWYs.

———. "Caring without Candor Should Raise Concerns." *The Growth and Resilience Network* (blog). October 13, 2013. stevepiscitelli.wordpress.com/2013/10/13/177-caring-without-candor-should-raise-concerns/.

———. "Did You Make a Difference? How Do You Know?" *The Growth and Resilience Network* (blog). April 12, 2015. stevepiscitelli.wordpress.com/?s=syllabus+review.

———. "The First Day of Class: People before Paper." *Innovation Abstracts.* NISOD 37.13, April 24, 2015.

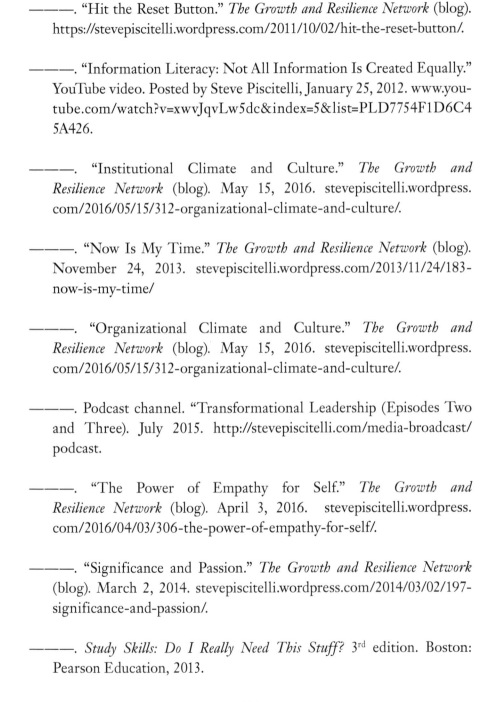

———. "Hit the Reset Button." *The Growth and Resilience Network* (blog). https://stevepiscitelli.wordpress.com/2011/10/02/hit-the-reset-button/.

———. "Information Literacy: Not All Information Is Created Equally." YouTube video. Posted by Steve Piscitelli, January 25, 2012. www.youtube.com/watch?v=xwvJqvLw5dc&index=5&list=PLD7754F1D6C45A426.

———. "Institutional Climate and Culture." *The Growth and Resilience Network* (blog). May 15, 2016. stevepiscitelli.wordpress.com/2016/05/15/312-organizational-climate-and-culture/.

———. "Now Is My Time." *The Growth and Resilience Network* (blog). November 24, 2013. stevepiscitelli.wordpress.com/2013/11/24/183-now-is-my-time/

———. "Organizational Climate and Culture." *The Growth and Resilience Network* (blog). May 15, 2016. stevepiscitelli.wordpress.com/2016/05/15/312-organizational-climate-and-culture/.

———. Podcast channel. "Transformational Leadership (Episodes Two and Three). July 2015. http://stevepiscitelli.com/media-broadcast/podcast.

———. "The Power of Empathy for Self." *The Growth and Resilience Network* (blog). April 3, 2016. stevepiscitelli.wordpress.com/2016/04/03/306-the-power-of-empathy-for-self/.

———. "Significance and Passion." *The Growth and Resilience Network* (blog). March 2, 2014. stevepiscitelli.wordpress.com/2014/03/02/197-significance-and-passion/.

———. *Study Skills: Do I Really Need This Stuff?* 3rd edition. Boston: Pearson Education, 2013.

———. "The Story of the Lavender Farmer." *The Growth and Resilience Network* (blog). October 18, 2015. stevepiscitelli.wordpress. com/2015/10/18/282-the-story-of-the-lavender-farmer/

———. "Transformational Leadership." *The Growth and Resilience Network* (blog). March 15, 2015. stevepiscitelli.wordpress. com/2015/03/15/251-transformational-leadership/.

———. "Trigger Warnings." *The Growth and Resilience Network* (blog). October 4, 2015. stevepiscitelli.wordpress.com/2015/10/04/280-trigger-warnings/.

———. "We Teach Much More than Our Disciplines," *Innovation Abstracts.* NISOD 37.27, November 13, 2015.

Popken, Ben. "College Textbook Prices Have Risen 1,041 Percent since 1977." *NBC News.* August 6, 2015.

Protheroe, Nancy. "Teacher Efficacy: What Is It and Does It Matter?" *Principal.* National Association of Elementary School Principals. May/June 2008: 42–45.

Rath, Tom, and Jim Harter. *Wellbeing: The Five Essential Elements.* New York: Gallup, 2010.

Resources: The 411 on All Things Mentoring Related. "The Differences between Coaching and Mentoring," http://www.management-mentors.com/resources/coaching-mentoring-differences, accessed November 14, 2016.

Sandler, Greg. "Four Effective Strategies for Managing Committees." *Higher Ed Jobs.* January 20, 2016, https://www.higheredjobs.com/Articles/articleDisplay.cfm?ID=806&Title=Four%20Effective%20Strategies%20for%20Managing%20Committees.

Schwartz, Tony. *The Way We're Working Isn't Working.* New York: Free Press, 2010.

Sharp, Eric. "The First Page of Google, by the Numbers." Protofuse. April 30, 2014.

Siebert, Al. *The Resiliency Advantage.* San Francisco, CA: Barrett-Koehler, 2005.

———. *The Survivor Personality.* New York: Penguin, 2010.

Slavov, Sita. "How to Fix College Grade Inflation." *US News and World Report.* December 26, 2013.

Stanoyevitch, Alexander. "Controlling Grade Inflation." *Thought and Action.* Fall 2008. http://www.nea.org/assets/img/PubThoughtAndAction/TAA_08_10.pdf.

Strang, Tami. "Four Types of Students You May See in Your Classroom." *Cengage Learning* (blog). January 14, 2014. http://blog.cengage.com/top_blog/four-types-of-students-you-may-see-in-your-classroom/.

Urban, Hal. *The Ten Commandments of Common Sense: Wisdom from the Scriptures for People of All Beliefs.* New York: Simon and Shuster, 2007.

Weimer, Maryellen, "First Day of Class Activities that Create a Climate of Learning." *Faculty Focus* (blog). January 9, 2013.

———. "Why Students Don't Attend Office Hours." *Faculty Focus* (blog). January 21, 2015.

ENDNOTES

1 To hear or read about Tony Hsieh's vision of collisions, type his name and *collisions* into your favorite search engine for more information. Also, see his book *Delivering Happiness: A Path To Profits, Passion, And Purpose* (New York: Business Plus, 2010).

2 For more on this analogy, see (among other sources) "Build Team and Trust and You'll Succeed, Duke's Coach 'K' Says in Ubben Lecture." *DePauw News and Media.* September 12, 2002. Also see, Tim Patron, "From the Court to the Classroom: The 'Fist' Team Analogy." *Duke Master of Management Student Blog.* February 14, 2014.

3 Steve Piscitelli, "We Teach Much More Than Our Disciplines," *Innovation Abstracts.* NISOD 37.27, November 13, 2015.

4 Principles of success are not new. A great deal of research and writing is available. You may want to review A. W. Chickering and Z. F. Gamson, "Seven Principles of Good Practice in Undergraduate Education," *American Association for Higher Education* Fall (1987): 2–6; Susan Rickey Hatfield, *The Seven Principles in Action: Improving Undergraduate Education* (Bolton, MA: Anker, 1995); Joe Cuseo, Viki S. Fecas, and Aaron Thompson, *Thriving in College & Beyond: Research-Based Strategies for Academic Success & Personal Development* (Dubuque, IA: Kendall/Hunt. 2016); and Joe Cuseo, "The 'Big Picture': Key Causes of Student Attrition & Key Components of a Comprehensive Student Retention Plan," December 2010, https://www.researchgate. net/publication/237318088_The_BIG_PICTURE_Key_Causes_ of_Student_Attrition_Key_Components_of_a_Comprehensive_ Student_Retention_Plan.

5 Steve Piscitelli, "The First Day of Class: People Before Paper." *Innovation Abstracts.* NISOD 37.16, April 24, 2015.

6   Steve Piscitelli, "Now Is My Time," *The Growth and Resilience Network* (blog), November 24, 2013, stevepiscitelli.wordpress.com/2013/11/24/183-now-is-my-time/.

7   I was initially turned on to this reflective idea by the work of Hal Urban, *The Ten Commandments of Common Sense: Wisdom from the Scriptures for People of All Beliefs* (New York: Simon and Shuster, 2007).

I have since found similar emphasis in the work of Tony Schwartz, *The Way We're Working Isn't Working.* (New York: Free Press, 2010). Also, when it comes to time invested and what we value, don't forget about the benefits of sleep for memory and learning. See, for example, Gordon B. Feld and Susanne Diekelmann, "Sleep Smart: Optimizing Sleep for Declarative Learning and Memory," *Frontiers in Psychology,* May 12, 2015.

8   Daniel Coyle, *The Little Book of Talent* (New York: Bantam Books, 2012), Tip #1.

9   See "About Wellness," National Wellness Institute, http://www.nationalwellness.org/?page=AboutWellness, accessed November 14, 2016. For different categorical labels for multiple dimensions of life, see Tom Rath and Jim Harter, *Wellbeing: The Five Essential Elements* (New York: Gallup, 2010).

10 Steve Piscitelli, "Hit The Reset Button," *The Growth and Resilience Network* (blog), October 2, 2011, https://stevepiscitelli.wordpress.com/2011/10/02/hit-the-reset-button/.

11 This story first appeared as Steve Piscitelli, "The Story of the Lavender Farmer," *The Growth and Resilience Network* (blog), October 18, 2015, https://stevepiscitelli.wordpress.com/2015/10/18/282-the-story-of-the-lavender-farmer/.

12 Steve Piscitelli, "Are You Relevant?," *The Growth and Resilience Network* (blog), November 8, 2015, https://stevepiscitelli.wordpress.com/2015/11/08/.

13 See Bernadette Jiwa, *Meaningful: A Story of Ideas that Fly* (Australia: Perceptive, 2015), Kindle edition, location 198. She also challenges us with "What happens because your product exists?" (Kindle Version, location 231.) Perhaps we should consider this in education: What happens because our school, campus, program, course, and/or section exists?

14 For discussion of this critical thinking model, see Steve Piscitelli, *Study Skills: Do I Really Need This Stuff?* 3rd edition (Boston: Pearson Education, 2013).

15 For a listing of a few such categories, see Honolulu Community College, "Faculty Development: Teaching Tips Index," http://www.honolulu.hawaii.edu/facdev/guidebk/teachtip/teachtip.htm accessed November 14, 2016. Also, see Joyce Povlacs Lunde, "101 Things You Can Do in the First Three Weeks of Class," University of Nebraska-Lincoln, Office of Graduate Studies, http://www.unl.edu/gradstudies/current/teaching/first-3-weeks, accessed November 14, 2016.

16 In addition to the continual growth of available information, the US Census Bureau reports expanding Internet usage and computer ownership. See Thom File and Camille Ryan, "Computer and Internet Use in the United States: 2013," *American Community Survey Reports*, U. Census Bureau, November 2014, https://www.census.gov/history/pdf/2013computeruse.pdf.

17 Steve Piscitelli, "Information Literacy: Not All Information Is Created Equally," *The Growth and Resilience Network* (blog), January 25, 2012, https://stevepiscitelli.wordpress.com/2012/01/29/

information-literacy-not-all-information-is-created-equally/. This blog post also includes a video: Steve Piscitelli, "Information Literacy: Not All Information Is Created Equally," YouTube video. Posted by Steve Piscitelli, January 25, 2012, www.youtube.com/watch?v=xwvJqv Lw5dc&index=5&list=PLD7754F1D6C45A426.

18 A recent Google search (November 12, 2016) by the author of the phrase "marketing and first page search engine results" yielded more than eight million hits. Also see Eric Sharp, "The First Page of Google, by the Numbers," Protofuse, April 30, 2014.

19 For a thorough review of how reflective practice can be applied to the classroom, see Stephen D. Brookfield, *Becoming a Critically Reflective Teacher* (San Francisco, CA: John Wiley and Sons, 1995).

20 Sylvia Hurtado, et al. Higher Education Research Institute at UCLA, "Undergraduate Teaching Faculty: The 2010–2011 HERI Faculty Survey," 2012, pp. 3-4.

21 Steve Piscitelli, "Awareness, Assumptions, and Actions. Why Do You Do What You Do?" YouTube Video. A TEDx-FSCJ talk, November 3, 2014. https://www.youtube.com/watch?v=HZQ2GEhoWYs.

22 For an incisive analysis of how the right questions at the right time can help us gain clarity, see Warren Berger, *A More Beautiful Question: The Power of Inquiry to Spark Breakthrough Ideas* (New York: Bloomsbury, 2014).

23 Al Siebert, *The Survivor Personality* (New York: Penguin, 2010).

24 Piscitelli, "We Teach Much More Than Our Disciplines."

25 For more on vulnerability, see Brené Brown, *Daring Greatly: How the Courage to be Vulnerable Transforms the Way We Live Love, Parent, and Lead* (New York: Gotham Books, 2012). Also, for a portrait of student characteristics that enter our classroom, see Arthur Levine and Diane R. Dean, *Generation on a Tightrope: A Portrait of Today's College Student* (San Francisco, CA: John Wiley and Sons, 2012). Also, see Chickering and Gamson, "Seven Principles of Good Practice in Undergraduate Education."

26 Al Siebert, *The Resiliency Advantage* (San Francisco, CA: Barrett-Koehler, 2005), 113.

27 Scott Jaschik, "Grade Inflation, Higher and Higher," *Inside Higher Ed*, March 29, 2016, https://www.insidehighered.com/news/2016/03/29/survey-finds-grade-inflation-continues-rise-four-year-colleges-not-community-college. Also see Sita Slavov, "How to Fix College Grade Inflation," *US News and World Report*, December 26, 2013.

28 Alexander Stanoyevitch, "Controlling Grade Inflation," *Thought and Action*, Fall 2008, http://www.nea.org/assets/img/PubThoughtAnd-Action/TAA_08_10.pdf.

29 Travis Andersen, "Harvard Professor Says Grade Inflation Rampant," BostonGlobe.com, December 4, 2013, accessed November 10, 2016.

30 Steve Piscitelli, "Caring Without Candor Should Raise Concerns," *The Growth and Resilience Network* (blog), October 13, 2013, https://stevepiscitelli.wordpress.com/2013/10/13/177-caring-without-candor-should-raise-concerns/.

31 Raymonda Burgman, "Avoiding Queen Bee Syndrome," *Inside Higher Ed*, April 20, 2016, https://www.insidehighered.com/advice/2016/04/20/how-deal-conflict-mentorship-experience-essay.

32 One example of a higher-education faculty mentoring program can be found at Calhoun Community College in Alabama (www.calhoun. edu). Under the auspices of the Director of Faculty Development, this mentoring program creates a new faculty cohort that collaborates and grows together for a three-year period. At the end of the three years, these cohort colleagues will then become mentors for new faculty at that time.

33 I saw this demonstration at a workshop I facilitated about fifteen years ago. I do not remember who did it or where it originated. I did not create this—but I recognized a great teaching tool when I saw it.

34 Also see Tami Strang, "Four Types of Students You May See in Your Classroom," *Cengage Learning* (blog), January 14, 2014, http://blog. cengage.com/top_blog/four-types-of-students-you-may-see-in-your-classroom/.

35 John Lee, *The Anger Solution: The Proven Method for Achieving Calm and Developing Healthy, Long-Lasting Relationships* (Cambridge, MA: Da Capo Press, 2009), 126-149.

36 John M Grohol, "FOMO Addiction: The Fear of Missing Out," *World of Psychology* (blog), PsychCentral, April, 14, 2011, http://psychcentral. com/blog/archives/2011/04/14/fomo-addiction-the-fear-of-missing-out/. Also see Nicholas Carr, *The Shallows: What the Internet is Doing to Our Brains* (New York: W.W. Norton, 2011) as well as Levine and Dean, *Generation on a Tightrope.*

37 The College Board, "Quick Guide: College Costs," Big Future, https://bigfuture.collegeboard.org/pay-for-college/college-costs/quick-guide-college-costs, accessed November 11, 2016.

38 Ben Popken, "College Textbook Prices Have Risen 1,041 Percent since 1977," NBC News, August 6, 2015.

39 Greg Sandler, "Four Effective Strategies for Managing Committees," *Higher Ed Jobs*, January 20, 2016, https://www.higheredjobs.com/Articles/articleDisplay.cfm?ID=806&Title=Four%20Effective%20Strategies%20for%20Managing%20Committees.

40 Also see Rusty Carpenter, "An Innovative Plan for Assessing Faculty Development," New Forums, May 4, 2016, http://newforums.com/an-innovative-plan-for-assessing-faculty-development/. This article presents two simple questions: What was learned and what will be implemented as a result of the development opportunity?

41 Over the years, I have seen and used (as a participant and a facilitator) many surveys, assessments and tools to gauge the impact of training. These two instruments combine elements from these various (and now unknown) conference and workshop sessions.

42 Siebert, *The Resiliency Advantage.*

43 Steve Piscitelli, "Transformational Leadership," *The Growth and Resilience Network* (blog), March 15, 2015, https://stevepiscitelli.wordpress.com/2015/03/15/251-transformational-leadership/. Also see Piscitelli's podcast channel for two episodes on transformational leadership: "Transformational Leadership (Episodes Two and Three), July 2015, http://stevepiscitelli.com/media-broadcast/podcast.

44 Steve Piscitelli, "Organizational Climate and Culture," *The Growth and Resilience Network* (blog), May 15, 2016, https://stevepiscitelli.wordpress.com/2016/05/15/312-organizational-climate-and-culture/.

45 Maryellen Weimer, "Why Students Don't Attend Office Hours," *Faculty Focus*, January 21, 2015.

46 See Hsieh, *Delivering Happiness: A Path to Profits, Passion, and Purpose* for more detail about the core principles of Zappos.

47 Nancy Protheroe, "Teacher Efficacy: What Is It and Does It Matter?," *Principal*, National Association of Elementary School Principals, May/June 2008: 42–45.

48 Examine Daniel Goleman's videos and writings about empathy. One place to start is at his website where you can find "Empathy 101," October 13, 2013, http://www.danielgoleman.info/empathy-101/.

49 Steve Piscitelli, "The Power of Empathy for Self," *The Growth and Resilience Network blog)*, April 3, 2016, https://stevepiscitelli.wordpress.com/2016/04/03/306-the-power-of-empathy-for-self/.

50 John Medina, *Brain Rules: 12 Principles for Surviving and Thriving at Work, Home, and School* (Seattle, WA: Pear, 2008).

51 Levine and Dean, *Generation on a Tightrope*.

52 Nicholas Carr, Chapter 7, "The Juggler's Brain," in *The Shallows: What the Internet is Doing to Our Brains* (New York: W.W. Norton, 2011).

53 Stephen D Brookfield, *Becoming a Critically Reflective Teacher* (San Francisco, CA: John Wiley and Sons, 1995), 114.

54 Steve Piscitelli, "Trigger Warnings," *The Growth and Resilience Network* (blog), October 4, 2015, https://stevepiscitelli.wordpress.com/2015/10/04/280-trigger-warnings/.

55 Tori DeAngelis, "Unmasking 'Racial' Micro Aggressions," *American Psychological Association* 40, no. 2 (2009): 42.

56 Caitlin Flanagan, "That's Not Funny!" *The Atlantic*, September 2015, http://www.theatlantic.com/magazine/archive/2015/09/thats-not-funny/399335/.

57 Greg Lukianoff and Jonathan Haidt, "The Coddling of the American Mind," *The Atlantic*, September 2015, http://www.theatlantic.com/magazine/archive/2015/09/the-coddling-of-the-american-mind/399356/.

58 Steve Piscitelli, "Institutional Climate and Culture," *The Growth and Resilience Network* (blog), May 15, 2016, accessed August 1, 2016, https://stevepiscitelli.wordpress.com/2016/05/15/312-organizational-climate-and-culture/.

59 Laura Guertin, "Getting Students to Read the Syllabus with a Syllabus Quiz," *AGU Blogosphere* (blog), AGU Blogosphere, August 27, 2014, http://blogs.agu.org/geoedtrek/2014/08/27/syllabus-quiz/.

60 Steve Piscitelli, "Did You Make A Difference? How Do You Know?" *The Growth and Resilience Network* (blog), April 12, 2015, https://stevepiscitelli.wordpress.com/?s=syllabus+review.

61 Steve Piscitelli, "Significance and Passion," *The Growth and Resilience Network* (blog), March 2, 2014, https://stevepiscitelli.wordpress.com/2014/03/02/197-significance-and-passion/.

62 Sean Blanda, "How to run Your Meetings Like Apple and Google," Behance: Empowering the Creative Community, http://99u.com/articles/7220/how-to-run-your-meetings-like-apple-and-google.

63 Sylvia Hurtado, et al., "Undergraduate Teaching Faculty: The 2010–2011 HERI Faculty Survey," Higher Education Research Institute at UCLA, Graduate School of Education and Information Studies, University of California, Los Angeles 2012, p. 4.

64 "The Differences Between Coaching and Mentoring," Resources: The 411 on All Things Mentoring Related, http://www.management-mentors.com/resources/coaching-mentoring-differences.

65 For one view see Adrienne LaFrance, "The Triumph of Email," *The Atlantic*, January 6, 2016, http://www.theatlantic.com/technology/archive/2016/01/what-comes-after-email/422625/.

66 As one example of faculty recognition, see the website of the National Institute for Staff and Organizational Development (NISOD) and its Excellence Awards. http://nisod.org/?q=products/excellence-awards, accessed November 14, 2016.

67 I first published this list in a 2015 article: Steve Piscitelli, "The First Day of Class: People Before Paper," *Innovative Abstracts*. NISOD 37.13, April 24, 2015.

68 Maryellen Weimer, "First Day of Class Activities that Create a Climate of Learning," *Faculty Focus* (blog). January 9, 2013.

Made in the USA
Charleston, SC
09 January 2017